Civility
in
America
Volume II

NEW ESSAYS FROM

AMERICA'S THOUGHT LEADERS

Sponsored by The Dilenschneider Group,
the City of Stamford, Connecticut, and Sacred Heart University.
Hosted in conjunction with Hearst Media Services CT and
The Ferguson Library, Stamford.

Significance Press
200 Park Avenue, 26th Floor
New York, NY 10166

ISBN: 978-0-9907574-5-0

DEDICATION

To Joel Kurtzman, who personifies civility
every day of his life.

TABLE OF CONTENTS

INTRODUCTION

The pages of this book give a powerful answer to the question of what is happening to civility in America.

As civility appears to crumble around us and our society, people are thinking seriously about how they contribute to decorum, respect and courtesy in their work and in their lives. They are asking themselves if they do enough, and they are seeking a forward-looking answer that means civility will be better served tomorrow than today, and even better the day after.

Such thought and resolve are major steps in assuring that civility remains one of our core values, and that we always advance its cause in our words and deeds. The 12 distinguished, successful people who have shared their views with the world in this book foster civility in the course of their daily interactions. They are leaders who set the bar high for us all.

And they should be heard by other leaders of our society who may not always set the examples we need. The lack of civility shown by so many prominent people, people who should know better but don't – or who simply don't care – insults the rest of us and inevitably leads to the rise of further incivility in our world.

We will hear in these pages from leaders in education, public safety, business, broadcast journalism, the arts, professional sports. All of them show us how to see and appreciate the effect of civility in fields with which we may not be familiar. They teach us how little acts of civility so positively influence the broader course of events.

We should learn from them that there is nothing so trivial, so outrageous, so insulting or distasteful, that we cannot react civilly and rise above the temptation to achieve momentary satisfaction by responding in kind. Instead, as these essays inform us, showing respect for others and treating them with dignity increases our respect for ourselves and raises the level of civility for everyone.

All of us can no doubt cite many more notable examples of incivility than of its opposite – we are exposed to it everywhere. But we can look to those who set a good example and take it to heart. We can behave as we know we should, and hold our heads high with the firm knowledge that when we act and react appropriately, we make a contribution to the betterment of our world.

Books are usually dedicated to one individual and we cited Joel Kurtzman. However, we also want to recognize the work of an amazing group of men, including Michael Novak; the late Cardinal Avery Dulles, S.J.; Cardinal Theodore E. McCarrick, Ph.D., D.D.; Joel I. Klein; F. Russell Hittinger, Ph.D.; Archbishop Celestino Migliore; Rev. John I. Jenkins, C.S.C.; Carl A. Anderson; Rev. Robert F. O'Toole, S.J.; Rev. Jeffrey von Arx, S.J.; William McGurn; John H. Garvey; Dr. Allan Goodman; and Rev. Michael Garanzini, who have shared their time and talents to shape the lives of thousands of younger men at St. Charles Preparatory School in Columbus, Ohio, through their civility, integrity and power of example.

Robert L. Dilenschneider.

Fay Vincent

on

Civility in Sports

You love baseball. And I love baseball, too. This little talk is about sports and civility, but I'm going to focus it on baseball. I know baseball best, and I'll start with a question that I will leave unanswered, and that is, if we're going to talk about civility and sports, let me ask you to think just for a minute about which sport has the least amount of trash-talking. I won't answer the question.

I'm going to do honor to my great friend "Bart" Giamatti, so this talk tonight starts and ends with the Romans. What Bart Giamatti would have done tonight is what I'm going to do in his honor. He would say, let's take the word "civility" and think about it. Where did it come from? The word "civility" comes from a Latin word – surprise, surprise – "civitas," which is the Latin word for "city" because, if you think about it, a city has to be a place of civil behavior; you can't have a city without rules, you can't have a city without laws.

So the Romans gave us this remarkable heritage, which is to collect citizens into a community. They are civilians. They will behave civilly because that is the law. And from the Romans, we have the concept of civil behavior.

Think of leaving here tonight and finding that all the red lights were out, and we were going to operate in a community without laws, without rules, so that on the way home at the four corners everybody would stop and the truck would go first, because the truck is the biggest, and all the rest of us would have to figure out how the hell we get across the intersection.

From the Romans, we have a concept of civility, but civility is premised on law in the city context. It is the law which organizes behavior and that permits collegial activities. Life depends on civility!

And when we turn to a game, what makes a game? Bart would think about this, and from him I think about it. You think about it. A game is something that takes place according to rules. Without rules, there cannot be a game. You can't have a contest unless someone says, these are the rules of the contest. There are no games in the jungle. If people race in the jungle, it's because they want to race. There are no rules about how long the race is, what you get if you win, what happens to you if you lose.

So, again, thinking about baseball and sports, the essence of sports, indeed, the essence of all games, whether it's chess or baseball or football or basketball, is a set of rules. And that's why those of us who are in the administration of sports, or were, or even the managers or, for that matter, the leaders of

2

players, everybody knows that the rules are important. And that means cheating, or fudging on the rules, is as important a threat to the game as lawless behavior is a threat to any city or any civilization.

Civitas, it is the concept of order based on law, and the game is a game because the rules tell you who plays it, how many. After all, everybody would like an extra shortstop, but the rules say no. Everybody would like a catcher's mitt three times bigger than the one they use. The rules say no. Everybody would like to put stuff on the baseball or cut it. Everybody would like a bigger first baseman's mitt. All sorts of things that have been tried, in the form of cheating.

And people say to me often, why is there such focus on cheating? Well, there's focus on cheating because if you permit cheating, you kill the game. The reason the steroid threat is serious, the reason Pete Rose - and betting on baseball – are serious issues is because they're existential threats to the game. They go to the heart of what the game is all about.

If you don't enforce the rules or you enforce them vaguely or intermittently, or you say we're not going to prevent some guy to load up a baseball because we think that's funny and we think spitballs or some sort of grease on the baseball is not a serious problem, the reason it's serious is the same reason that a little bit of tax cheating is serious.

The reason you can't have people cheat up to 10 percent of their income or steal 10 percent of what they can steal is because the 10 percent leads to greater thefts. The problem with sports is that if you permit a little cheating, pretty soon you have widespread cheating.

For me, and I think for you, the concept of civility is not a luxury. It's not a form of manners or politesse. It's absolutely essential to the preservation and joy of the game. If we can't trust the rules and the enforcers, the managers and the commissioners, and others, we can't trust the game. And then we'll have – excuse me - professional wrestling.

Or we'll have movies. We'll have entertainment. But the difference between entertainment and sports is rules. And it's that simple.

Civility is not something that I come to you and say is a matter of sort of gloss on the game. It's not people being polite, though that may be part of it – and I'll come to that in a minute. It's really at the heart of what baseball is all about.

And, if you think about it when you watch a game, there are some things that will get you instantly dismissed from the game. It happens. Even good men, such as some of those present, have on occasion been invited to the showers prematurely.

And I once said to my good friend Bruce Froemming, 35 years an umpire in the Big Leagues, I said to him, "Brucie, what is it that a player has to say to you that will get you tossed out of a game? What are the magic words?"

I mean, I've heard about the magic words. Now listen to his – this is a very bright man. I talked to him today. I told him I was going to cite his answer.

He said to me, "Commissioner, anything with the word 'you' in front of it."

Now, if you think about that, the word "you" in front of a bad word will do it. If I say to Brucie, "That was a bad call, Brucie," that's okay, you can say that. If you question his mother's lineage – all right, then you've gone too far.

4

So I said to him one day, "Brucie, all the years you're umpiring, I want to know, who came to you and gave you a shot that was so good and so clever that you couldn't say anything, and you couldn't throw him out?" I said, "What's the best shot you ever took from a ballplayer?"

Well, he said, "That's an easy one. I'm in St. Louis, it's about 1,000 degrees. I have the plate, and Tom Seaver's pitching against Bob Gibson. Now they're Hall of Fame pitchers and they're putting the ball a half inch on the black for a strike and a half inch off the black, and I'm calling it a ball. And they think those are two similar and equal pitches. When he's on the black, he gets the strike. I'm not giving him the pitch off the black. that's the way it is. That's the rule."

And Bruce says, "Seaver's stalking around but he doesn't say anything. Gibson is getting hot 'cause I won't give him the pitch off the black. I call a couple of balls on him, the inning ends and he walks off the mound, and he takes a little detour toward the plate. He's careful because if he goes too far, I'm going to walk away and tell them to get lost. And over his shoulder as he walks toward the dugout, he says to me, 'Froemming, you're better than that.'"

Now, Bruce said, "What the hell am I gonna say? I said, have a good day."

Let me get to Pete Rose. It's one thing to violate a rule on the field, to cheat, that's bad. But if you do what Rose did, you get yourself thrown out for life. What did he do? Well, he bet on baseball. He was corrupt. He corrupted the game. And that's a serious crime. That's the top crime in baseball.

And why is the Pete Rose case important? It's important because that was, again, a threat to the game, and he posed it because he believed he was above the rules. And he thought that because he was this great player, Hall of Fame player, he could do what he pleased, and Bart Giamatti, the Commissioner, would back off and not go after him.

Well, we went after him. I wrote the agreement. He signed it. And he's out of baseball for life. And there's no redemption. You know, I'm a nice little Catholic boy, and the Catholic Church is premised on forgiveness and redemption. Baseball is not. There is no redemption in baseball. You can't earn your way back, once you've done what Pete Rose did.

But here's the point I want you to think about. It's not about Pete Rose. This is about the deterrent. The reason there's no gambling in baseball is Pete Rose. Everyone knows that if you get caught, whether you're Ralph Branca or Bobby Valentine or Fay Vincent, if you get caught, you are out of baseball for life, and you are not coming back.

The argument to me is not that Pete Rose earned his way back, that he suffered, that he did penance, that he should be redeemed. The issue is who is going to take the chance that by bringing Pete Rose back you undermine that deterrent, you make it tolerable for players to say, "I'm a great player, I'm likely to be every bit as good as Pete Rose, I'm a Hall of Fame player?"

Tom Seaver said to me, "If you bring Rose back, aren't you telling me, Tom Seaver, that I can bet on baseball, because you're saying if I'm good enough to win all the games I won as Tom Seaver, I can behave in such a fashion, knowing that down the road the public, bless its heart, will say, bring Tom back. He's a good guy. He bet on baseball, but he's not a bad person. He shouldn't be punished for life."

That deterrent is really important. And I defend it and I think that if you think about it, I think you will agree with me.

Let's go back to civility on the field. I'm going to give you three little examples of tiny aspects of civility that you might not have seen. Or you've seen them, but you may not have realized what's going on. When you see a batter foul off a pitch and hit the catcher in the throat, in the shoulder, wherever the catcher's hurt, the catcher will go down, the umpire will bend over him and the catcher will gradually come out of it.

Then the umpire will immediately brush off home plate, slowly and carefully. The umpire will then, very slowly, walk to the mound with the ball. And he will hand the ball to the pitcher. He could have thrown it. What's he doing? He's stalling. Your eyes are following him out to the mound. You're not saying, hey, come on, let's go, catcher, let's get on with it.

The umpire is very civilly, I submit to you, and very nicely giving that catcher a minute to come back. And when he comes back, he'll dust the plate off again, just to be sure, and then the catcher will get back in and the game will go on. You've seen it, but I invite you to think about it, in terms of what's really going on. It's a very nice little civilizing touch.

All of us who've been around baseball know it happens. The umpire will do it just as a matter of courtesy. They have not been told to do it, but they want to do it. They know the catcher's stunned, and they want to give him a break.

Here is one I'm pretty sure you don't know. All of you think of yourselves as reasonably knowledgeable baseball fans. I'm going to show you a signal that takes place on the field fairly often.

The batter in the batter's box, usually left-handed, taps the top of his head. Now, before this session, I put this to two distinguished baseball people. One of them had the answer.

The answer is that happens when the batter is left-handed and the pitcher is left-handed – there's a runner on first - and as the batter is looking at the pitcher, the umpire at second base is in the line of sight of the batter, as he looks at the left-handed pitcher. So he touches the top of his head. That is a generally-accepted message: "Mr. Umpire at second base, would you mind getting the hell out of my line of sight?"

Now, it's a civil request. There's no rule. There's nothing that says the umpire can't say a rude word – or "I'm not moving." The umpire will move. And he usually will move from the second baseman side to the shortstop side to get out of the line of sight. Or he may move behind second base. But he'll move.

And Wade Boggs, Hall of Famer who played for the Red Sox, must have done this a thousand times in his career. He just couldn't stand having that umpire in his line of sight. But I'm pretty certain that most of you haven't noticed. You will now because you'll see the batter back out and he'll do that, and the umpire will move. It happens, and it's one of the many things that go on in a ballgame that you might miss.

The last one you never miss, and that is the poor catcher. A batter hits a popup behind home plate, the catcher throws off his mask, turns around, chases the ball. The ball goes in the seats and the catcher comes back and, of course, his mask is in the dust.

I would say 90 times out of 100 the batter will pick up the mask and hand it to catcher. Again, a very tiny little civilizing moment, but it's one of those things that makes baseball different. You almost never see that in football. You'll never see it in hockey. And it puts baseball in a slightly different category.

Finally, let me talk to you about uncivil behavior, or behavior that's lacking in civility. And I come to you as the son of a former NFL official. When I was a kid, my father was an official in the NFL, so I grew up in a family where people who refereed sports, to me, were heroes. My father! How could you be a bigger hero than my father?

And so, when people yelled, as they often did, when he was doing a baseball game, "Kill the umpire," I thought, wait a minute, the umpire's my father. Why would you say that? That's pretty awful. And nobody means it, any more than they mean the abuse they heave on any official.

But think about what's taking place. We're teaching kids. We're in the stands, we're screaming at the umpire at first base for missing a call or some other foolish thing that got the audience in an uproar. There's something really damaging about that. It's corrosive, because baseball is a generational sport. We usually bring kids with us. We're teaching kids behavior.

And when we coach a little league team and we scream at the balls and strikes and we scream at an official, what are we doing? Why are we doing that? Are we aware of what's really taking place? We're transmitting lessons. We're teaching. We're doing things that are basically uncivilized. And that's why it's so dangerous and so corrosive.

For me, there is no excuse for abusing an umpire. My father would come home after a game, a football game, and he knew if he missed a call, and he would be literally ill. He felt awful, for days. On Wednesday, Thursday, I'd say, "How are you?" "Well," he said, "I'm still mad about that lousy call, that I missed it." He said, "I just missed it." I realized he took it very seriously, and he was more upset than anybody on the field that day. He was very, very down about it.

I'm going to leave you with the concept that rules are important because they define the game. Civilized behavior means adherence to rules. The little civilities in baseball are important because they're acknowledging something very important, which is that there is meaning beyond the pitch or the game.

What the players are doing, although they don't know they're doing it, is they're sending messages about values. And, to some extent, it's that value system that we all have to be worried about.

In this country, we have a mess on our hands because we can't agree on values. We're not sure what immoral conduct means. Think about it, if I said to you, could we get a consensus in this room on immorality, we couldn't. Fifty years ago, there would have been no question about that consensus.

So we've lost our ability to decide what's right and what's wrong. I put crimes aside. We know what the law is, but short of the law, when we're talking right and wrong, we are in a mess. And that's a sad reality. It shows up in sports.

But, again, I think the reason sports is so important - and bless baseball - baseball does stand for some things. In some respects, baseball's alone. It says there's no fudging about cheating. There's no situation ethics. You can't tell us because it's raining hard it's okay to cheat, or because it's cold or because you're sick – there are no excuses in baseball. It's a perfect meritocracy, and the value system is really important.

Allan E. Goodman

on

Civility Through International Education:
On Making the World a Less Dangerous Place

T he daily headlines remind us constantly of the many things that are not working in our own society's public discourse. And in a recent article entitled "Can America be Fixed?" (January/February 2013, Foreign Affairs), Fareed Zakaria notes, in fact, that "Studies show that the political divisions in Washington are at their worst since the years following the Civil War."

Because the Institute of International Education works in the realm of public diplomacy and international educational exchange, allow me to offer a few reflections on how all this is affecting how we are seen in the world.

While I do live in Washington and have taught at Georgetown, I am here to make the point that the lack of civility is not only an inside-the-Beltway problem. The idea behind the founding of our Institute in 1919 was that if people in the academic professions in different countries got to know each other better, it would eventually eliminate war. Neither we nor the world have yet achieved that.

And we are also in the business of rescuing scholars who are harassed and persecuted by governments and terrorists alike. While we have also been doing this since our founding in 1919, over 4,000 from 100 countries have applied to us for help since we endowed the Institute's Scholar Rescue Fund in 2002. Academic freedom in all-too-many places and situations becomes a matter not only of protecting free speech and thinking, but also of saving lives.

And across our worldwide presence, I have been struck by how polarized public discourse is becoming, how many demagogues in high office there are, how much media and fundamentalist audiences crave conspiracy theories to account for what is going on and demonize those whom they oppose. Speaking out or challenging conventional wisdom or orthodoxy on virtually any subject appears to be increasingly risky in many places.

So there is plenty of bad news about the absence of civility, and on a global scale.

But I am not going to dwell on any of it. My aim is to make the opposite case by describing how civility plays out when it works through educational exchange programs like Fulbright, which the Institute has the honor to administer on behalf of the U.S. Department of State. Indeed, I actually have some good news to share.

The late Senator J. William Fulbright often made the point that educational exchange "humanizes international relations by transforming nations into people." At its core, the program operationalizes what Plato and Cicero both found so important about civility; namely the qualities of *humanitas*, or treating others with respect, and *pietas*, the desire to act towards others out of charity.

Civility inspires both. And I encounter it practically every day in the work we do.

First, a bit of background about the Fulbright Program itself.

It remains, as the British historian Arnold Toynbee observed, "one of the really generous and imaginative things that have been done in the world since World War II." This was the forgiveness of debt for the victors as well as the vanquished. Toynbee knew that few nations ever do that.

The Senator succeeded in amending a law that allowed countries owing us money to keep the funds if they set them aside in an education account that would fund educational exchange so that future leaders and generations would better understand each other.

This act of World War II debt forgiveness essentially funded the whole Fulbright Program until 1961; since then, the Congress has provided an annual appropriation that now supports nearly 10,000 American and international students and scholars with the chance to get to know each other's society and values through a year or more of study in their respective countries.

The Program sends and receives academics from 150 different countries. The appropriation is supplemented by contributions from the private sector and over 100 other governments – even though we have differences with many over their foreign policies or ours.

Short of waging very popular wars (of which there are few), no other federal program or undertaking receives such international support. And war is a good budgetary comparator. The whole of the Fulbright Program since its beginning in 1946 up until the present has cost less than one week of what was spent on the war in Afghanistan in 2012.

What is the value of Fulbright and how does it contribute to civility? Allow me to share just three stories.

"I am studying to be an astronaut." The speaker was a Fulbright student at a luncheon with others on the program in the Alumni Room above the football stadium at the University of Colorado in Boulder. You could hear the practice calls and imagine the crowd that would soon fill the stadium below. What I suspect you cannot imagine is that the speaker was a student from Pakistan. UC Boulder is one of the nation's leading training grounds for astrophysicists and astronauts. It made sense that he wanted to be there and to be Islamabad's first man in outer space.

Nothing seemed to me more incongruent. He stood before us dressed in a flowing beige Khameez and spoke in a very high pitched voice – not at all like what we hear from the men who inhabit the space station or who stepped foot on the moon. And I thought to myself, "He is so different."

Mr. Khan shared a recent experience he had as a Fulbrighter meeting with others from around the world on the Program. "We gathered to explore our experiences and our differences. Each of my fellows went around the table describing where they hailed from and the peculiarities of their geography and culture. When it came to be my turn, I said that what I was learning is that we all want education, we all want a better world for our children, and we all want peace. So, to me and in fact, there really are no differences."

Instantly, I thought back to Senator Fulbright's point about transforming nations into people. It had, in fact, happened before my eyes.

It makes a difference to realize that there are no differences because that form of civility also promotes toleration and trust – actions that have to be profoundly grounded in charity and respect. Like me, many others will find themselves wondering – especially after watching "Zero Dark Thirty" – about whether or not we could or should ever work with people like Mr. Khan or from his country. The experience of hearing this future astronaut gave me hope. And

14

while hope is not a strategy, sometimes it is the only thing we actually have when surface differences seem so powerful as forces which divide us.

Another thing I am privileged to do is ask Fulbright Alumni what difference the Program and experience made to their lives. After all, those selected in such a competitive process ought to be fully capable of succeeding as they have without the Fellowship. What I am after is that "eureka moment" when something happens only because they were doing what they did on a Fulbright.

And so one evening I found myself seated at a dinner next to a very distinguished Japanese gentleman who had once been a Fulbright student in America. His answers to my question about what difference did it make surprised me.

"My father was a salaryman and worked for a large company. I imagined that this was what I would also do. But during my Fulbright years, I got to know many Americans who did things differently than their father did. And many who went from the private sector into government jobs. It was hard then for us Japanese to think of government work as honorable, so I was impressed that Americans thought this way."

"I returned from Tokyo with two great gifts from America. I decided that I would apply to work in the Ministry of Finance rather than the company where my father worked. And I met my wife there, who was also on a Fulbright."

There, I thought the story would end.

My companion, though, continued.

"I learned that American men listened to their wives and often let them pursue their own careers. So when we moved back, I encouraged my wife to do the same." Eventually, this Fulbrighter joined the UN and served as the world's High Commissioner for

Refugees. Her husband became the Governor of the Japan's Central Bank and guided the country out of a deep recession.

This type of civility – respect for what others and what people in other places do – empowers.

And then there is the aspect of civility that humanizes us all by teaching compassion. So, a final story.

Last year, my work took me to Beijing, where our office arranged a dinner with the American Fulbright students then in the middle of their China projects. Most were working or teaching at universities and libraries in the capitol or within an hour or two train ride away. The woman next to me, however, told me it had taken her two days to get to Beijing.

She explained that she is an environmental science graduate student from The Ohio State University, doing her Ph.D. on river water micro-organisms in Northwest China. Her field research project involved collecting samples in a very remote village. To get to Beijing, she told me, you had to take several busses, then a train, and finally an air flight. She assured me there were plenty of things in Chinese river water to analyze.

Naturally, I assumed she was in town to get some of her samples tested.

She said no and, in fact, had not brought any of her water with her. She had come to Beijing to try to arrange a surgery for a young girl in the village who was badly injured in a car crash. The father had been killed, the mother crippled, and the nine-year-old girl sustained many problematic head injuries.

Now this remote village rarely sees any outsiders. Perhaps this tall, blond, Buckeye from Ohio was the first American in the village's five thousand year history that had ever gone there. She is certainly someone they will never forget.

"What else could I do? If the girl did not get help, she would have absolutely no future. And no one would care for her when I left. And maybe I was the only person that could find a medical mission group that could help her. I can always collect water samples. This was Liang's only one chance, maybe, at living her life."

The more she talked about the situation, and as I reflect now on her uncanny resemblance to Anne Hathaway, this Ohio State Fulbrighter reminded me that Victor Hugo had a very fundamental point when he wrote in *Les Misérables* that, "to love another is to see the face of God."

Civility is important for many reasons. I encounter it almost every day through international education and I am glad to say that the world often sees us in ways differently than we see ourselves. The exchanges our Institute promotes on behalf of the Department of State and the Programs that Congress even today supports in a very bipartisan way may be the best investment any of us have to make the world we share a less dangerous place for little Liang – and for all who care about whether the next generation will be inclined to make war or peace.

Edward T. Reilly

on

Civility in Management

I am pleased to have the opportunity to explore with you the subject of civility in management. We deal with this issue quite often at the American Management Association, but to set the stage for our discussion, I thought it would be useful to establish what "civility" means. Most of us have an idea of what civil behavior looks like. Rooted in three thousand years of western civilization, to paraphrase Justice Potter Stewart, we know it when we see it.

Civil behavior might be defined as that which relates to citizens and their inter-relations with one another or with the state in accordance with organized society.

In reading the papers of the Founding Fathers, there is a general expectation that civil behavior is a pre-condition to liberty. My interpretation of their belief is that people should be free, free to behave as they wish--as long as they are respectful of others. In those days, the meaning of "respectful" seems to have been generally understood.

To continue with the civics lesson analogy, let me bring up the notion of the social compact. Again, a dictionary definition is roughly "the voluntary agreement among individuals by which, (according to any of the various theories –

Hobbs, Locke or Rousseau), organized society is brought into being and invested with the right to secure mutual protection and welfare or to regulate the relationship among its members". Why is civility important? It is essentially the rules by which we carry out our side of the social compact. So this civil behavior thing is pretty important stuff!

Most people learn the basic rules of behavior from their parents and their schools. Do you remember Robert Fulghum's popular book from years ago: "All I Really Need to Know I Learned in Kindergarten"? It turns out there's a lot of truth in that! When we abide by the generally accepted set of rules that we're exposed to early in life it creates the foundation for our behavior as adults. And the same rules of civility that apply when we're in kindergarten are no less important in business and management.

In general, if people are predisposed to behave civilly towards one another, there will be more freedom and fewer rules, and the society, or the company, will function more effectively. When you can "trust" that people will behave in an acceptable manner, the wheels of business are greased and you can move much more quickly. "Trust and verify" may be an appropriate policy for two super powers with very different agendas, but it sure slows things down among people with common goals.

In this series we'll be discussing civility as it pertains to many different aspects of our society; art, politics, law enforcement, education, international education, sports and of course, management. Each field has its own issues and its own expectations of what constitutes civil behavior.

After all, what is allowed in the National Football League – what might be defined as a "clean hit" – would hardly be considered civilized behavior on Metro North (at least not during off-peak hours) but there are great similarities in what is considered acceptable within different fields, and many of these fields are interrelated. My field of management, for example, depends heavily on the results of the education establishment, confidence in law enforcement, and the effective exercise of political dialog.

With regard to management, let me say that my views are from my own perceived wisdom, and not necessarily from the American Management Association. They have been formed by my interaction with parents and educators, and from over 30 years of experience in the private sector and more than ten fortunate years as head of the American Management Association. If I may indulge in a moment to boast about an organization of which I'm extremely proud:

The American Management Association is, I believe, a remarkable institution. We are a 90-year-old nonprofit organization, organized under a charter from the New York State Board of Regents as an institute of higher education. We train and develop managers throughout the United States and around the world.

Each year, we train more than 150,000 managers from thousands of companies, large and small, local and global. We conduct research and training, publish books, sponsor seminars and meetings, and our teaching curriculum divides the management world into more than 180 targeted programs which our nearly 800 faculty members teach around the world. We are centrally located to observe trends in business and help our members react accordingly.

It is from this vantage point that I have been able to observe the profound changes taking place in the world of business and the way business is conducted. Global competition, an increasingly diverse workforce, incredible advances in technology, and changed expectations of goods and services to feed our technologically-enhanced society have all led to profound changes in the ways organizations are structured and led.

Peter Drucker wisely observed that our world has become so complex that little of true value can be accomplished without the support of organizations. Medicine, the arts, education, material production and distribution and, of course, the food we eat, rarely get to us without close involvement of organizations—often large organizations—and all of those organizations have to be structured, managed and led.

There has been a clear shift away from the industrial-age command-and-control structure— designed to efficiently produce and distribute products—to a more collaborative structure where people of diverse backgrounds and diverse but complementary skills are brought together to operate in an information-intensive world to produce rapidly evolving goods and services. In this structure, leadership, as opposed to management, takes on a more prominent role.

It may sound heretical, coming from the president of the American Management Association, but I generally accept the premise that management, while an absolutely necessary skill, is insufficient on its own, for organizations to win. While nuts-and-bolts management is central to how much gets done and at what cost, to be successful in today's environment, effective leadership must be central to what and how things get done.

We offer many courses, books, webcasts, podcasts, etc. on leadership, leadership style and execution, but I think it is safe to say that in every offering, the ability to develop, articulate and gain commitment to a vision and mission is presented as an absolute necessity. People expect, and are expected to exercise a degree of freedom and initiative to help the organization accomplish its objectives. And it is important that they understand both these objectives and the culture within which they will operate.

So, just as the United States of America is the only country in the world united by ideas, not geography, companies are united by ideas and values and mission. In addition, virtually all organizations need unwritten rules, a code of conduct, a set of principles that are well understood by the participants: a set of common expectations.

In business, we generally refer to this as the company culture, or, more colloquially, the way we do things around here!

Most senior managers would agree that maintaining a civil or respectful workplace is essential, yet we are surrounded by evidence that what is preached is often not practiced. Consequently we have ample evidence that shows employees are dissatisfied with their leadership and frustrated by the behavior of some, and sometimes many of their fellow workers.

In a large survey we conducted recently, companies confirmed that the skills they believed were necessary to succeed in their organizations included the 4Cs: Communication, Creativity, Collaboration, and Critical Thinking. (I would also add to that list, Curiosity). But how can you expect clear, effective communication or world-class collaboration from a group of people who are used to behaving in uncivil, disrespectful ways towards one another?

So the answer would seem to be that we need to operate with fewer rules, but more effective behavior. We need to accomplish more; but was can't afford to rely on "trust and verify." We need to provide our associates at all levels with an environment that supports the behavior we expect of them, and doesn't stifle their energy or enthusiasm.

Most companies I know of are constantly in search of creativity and innovation – and they know it comes from a confident, energetic staff. While many companies of all sizes are effective at producing a civil, respectful workplace, it seems that the majority of workers in

America and around the world don't feel it happens in their particular organization.

Here are a few numbers from our survey that make the point:

- 60 percent of employees believe their fellow employees' annoying behavior negatively affects the workplace.

- A large proportion of employees are looking for a new job.

- 80 percent of employees claim they are treated uncivilly at work at least once a week.

- Three out of four employees are dissatisfied with the way their company handles incivility.

Clearly this is not what management/leadership wants. Many factors contribute to this situation. For example, in many ways, the workforce is far more diverse than it has ever been. As a result, I don't think people necessarily have similar backgrounds and the shared experiences might have been prevalent years ago. This makes misunderstandings and conflict more likely.

In addition, the past four years in the American workplace have been particularly difficult. Fewer people are doing more work under more pressure with fewer options and less control over their own careers and lives. We know that feeling a lack of control is one of the greatest producers of stress. And technology keeps many of us "on" 10 or more hours a day, often seen days a week. Instant communications technology leaves little time to review for politeness. There's a big difference between hitting "send" and signing a note that was dictated earlier, typed, and presented for review.

So what can we do to overcome these challenges? First, let me offer a working definition of the goal. The constant practice of behaviors. At AMA we offer courses that go a long way toward solving the problems. For example, we have been teaching a course called "How to Communicate with Diplomacy, Tact and Credibility." We h have another course aimed at building better work relationships that also stresses results-oriented communications.

We offer many seminars in leadership development, all of which highlight respect, implicitly or explicitly, in the program. Recently we introduced a program directly on point entitled, "Create a Respectful Workplace: Improve Morale, Increase Productivity and Achieve Business Goals." The course teaches participants, among other things:

1. How to create a working definition of workplace disrespect and incivility.

2. Tools for calculating the true costs of a disrespectful climate to the organization.

3. How to assess a manager's own actions and how those actions influence certain behaviors

4. How to coach employees to deal successfully with disrespectful situations before issues escalate.

5. The key actions that successful companies use to create respectful workplaces.

6. Strategies for building and for overcoming obstacles to building a positive, respectful climate.

From a business leadership point of view, management wants staff to be well satisfied so they can make greater contributions to the organization's mission. Many issues converge to make this objective challenging. Like other issues, it takes identifying the problem and making a firm commitment to consciously connect it to make changes. Wishing it were so is not a plan.

In the months and years ahead, this issue will be attracting more attention. As the economy finally begins to heal, and people regain a modicum of control over their careers and can change jobs when not happy, we will learn more about the extent of the dissatisfaction that exists.

Although it will take some time, I'm convinced that the advantages of investing in the effort to construct and maintain a more civil workplace will win out and good progress will be made. Meanwhile, I hope the other segments of our society, especially families and schools, find ways to pattern civil behavior in those for whom they are responsible, and that we make progress in this realm across all aspects of society. The payoff is too large to ignore.

Georgia Nugent

On

Civility and the Liberal Arts

A nationwide poll on Civility in America, conducted in August of 2013, found that 71 percent of respondents felt that civility has declined in recent years – and also that this situation is "the new normal." 54 percent believe civility will continue to decline. But we should not be complacent. How could this trend be halted? Certainly not with platitudes about being nice. I believe that, if we want to make a difference, we need to be more rigorous in our understanding of what we really mean by civility, how it is fostered, and why it matters to us.

I am a professor of Greek and Latin, a former college president, and a passionate believer in the value of liberal arts education – and I will draw upon each of these in my remarks tonight. First, I want to clarify what "civility" means—by tracing its ancient roots in Western culture and illustrating the centrality of that heritage in our own history. Second, I will explore the connections between the concept of civility and the fundamentally American practice of liberal arts education.

Frankly, there will be one unabashedly evangelical section of my talk. I will be drawing here on my current role as Senior Fellow at the Council of Independent Colleges (in Washington, D.C.). CIC is an association of more than 600 small, private liberal arts colleges, and we are embarking on a national campaign to better inform the public about the value and power of liberal arts education and liberal arts colleges. That campaign is entitled: "Sustaining America's Future: The Power of the Liberal Arts." I truly believe those two are integrally related, and, in my closing words to you tonight, I hope to make clear some of the reasons for that.

Let's begin with the term, "civility" itself. One of the great things about studying the so-called "dead" languages is that they aren't dead at all! They are astoundingly vital and vivid, everywhere around us.

So, for example, tonight...

We are in a **library** from the Latin *liber*, "book"

And we're in an **auditorium** from the Latin *audio*, "hear" or "listen"

This might have been a **symposium** from the Greek roots *syn*, "with" or "together," and *potis*, "drinking"—a symposium was, originally, a drinking party. (Sorry – that's not our format here tonight!)

And on, and on, and on. Not only in English but in all European languages, the roots of Greek and Latin are the very building blocks of the languages we speak every day, and, to that extent, they subtly shape the way we think. The study of these linguistic origins – etymology – can serve as a kind of x-ray, revealing and illuminating what lies beneath our everyday language and concepts.

And so it is with **civility**. Our English word is derived directly from the Latin word, *civis*, "citizen." This etymology tells us that the most fundamental meaning of civility is: "the quality of being a citizen." To understand the true grounding of our concept, then, we'll need to explore what being a citizen meant in antiquity.

Why should citizenship in the ancient past be relevant at all to our contemporary life in America? Well, not only because the vestiges of Greece and Rome live on in our language. But also because the Founders of our American republic self-consciously modeled this nation on their understanding of Greece and Rome. As the great American historian Gordon Wood has written about the Revolutionary period, classical learning "was not only a scholarly ornament of educated Americans; it helped to shape their values and their ideals of behavior." When we talk about "civility," surely we are talking about an "ideal of behavior." So it makes sense to think through what "civility" really means by trying to grasp what our forefathers might have gleaned about the ideal of civility from their classical learning.

In his important study, *The Founders and the Classics: Greece, Rome, and the American Enlightenment* (Harvard, 1994), Carl Richard notes that, "The founders …turned to the ancients for their models of government, most notably the Greek republics of the 5th and 4th centuries B.C. and the Roman republic from the 6th to 1st century B.C." As I said, our English word, "civility," comes to us directly from the Romans' language, Latin. But I am going to turn our attention tonight more directly to the democracy of 5th century Athens, because I think we can find there a unique – and uniquely compelling – embodiment of our subject.

The Greeks, too (of course) "had a word for it." Their term, the translation of *civilitas* into Greek (if you will), was *politeia*, stemming from the word for "the city" in Greek: *polis*. The very best way to understand what *polis* meant to the Greeks, I think, is to turn to

Aristotle's work "The Politics." "Man," Aristotle famously proclaims there, "is a political animal." Now by this, he doesn't mean that office politics around the water cooler is inevitable. Nor does he mean anything having to do with the Beltway, as we know it. No; in saying "man is a political animal," Aristotle means something much more fundamental. He means that it is the nature of human beings to live in a community (and for the Greeks that meant a city, a *polis*).

There has likely never been a more passionate believer in the *polis* than the Greek philosopher, Socrates. Aside from a brief – and courageous – stint of military service, Socrates never ventured outside the walls of his native Athens. Ultimately, he even gave up his life for this commitment to his city. Our knowledge of Socrates has come down to us mainly through his pupil, Plato. As far as we know, Socrates didn't write any works. But he was so extraordinary a figure that Plato (and several other contemporaries) wrote accounts of his life and teachings. And perhaps the most famous of these texts is Plato's "Apology."

The "Apology" is the account of Socrates' speech in his own defense, when he is put on trial for his life before the Athenian court. Two enemies of Socrates have brought the charge that he is "corrupting the youth" of Athens. The form this "corruption" allegedly takes is that the philosopher insists on hanging about in the central marketplace (the agora), questioning and testing young men's beliefs, prodding them to think deeply and clearly about what we would call today "the big questions": What is justice? What is the best form of government? What constitutes a good life? (As I will claim a little later, these are questions that we might associate today with liberal arts education. But we'll come back to that.)

These "big questions" – both then and now – may make people uncomfortable. We don't always <u>want</u> to question our beliefs; in today's jargon, it takes us "out of our comfort zone." But, frankly, Socrates isn't concerned about that. Toward the end of his defense, he speculates about what might happen if the court would acquit him, but with the proviso that he stop all his "philosophizing" and asking questions. What, then, would he do? Let me turn to the text itself:

"I should reply, Gentlemen, I am your very grateful and devoted servant, but…so long as I draw breath and have my faculties, I shall never stop practicing philosophy and exhorting you and elucidating the truth for everyone that I meet. I shall go on saying, in my usual way: 'My very good friend, you are an Athenian and belong to a city which is the greatest and most famous in the world for its wisdom and strength. Are you not ashamed that you devote your attention to acquiring as much money as possible, and similarly with reputation and fame, and give no attention or thought to truth and understanding and the perfection of your soul?'....I shall do this to everyone I meet, young or old, foreigner or fellow citizen, but especially to you, my fellow citizens, because you are dearer to me."

You know the verdict in this trial – Socrates is sentenced to be put to death by drinking the poison, hemlock. After learning the verdict, he has this to say:

"If I tell you that to let no day pass without discussing goodness and all the other subjects about which you hear me talking, examining myself and others, is really the very best thing that a man can do, and that life without this sort of examination is not worth living, you will be even less inclined to believe me. Nevertheless that is how it is, gentlemen, as I maintain, though it is not easy to convince you of it."

And so, rather than give up his practice of pursuing the truth, in dialogue with others, Socrates willingly goes to his death. Now, given his lofty ideals, why would his fellow citizens – for whom he professes so much concern – bring him to trial and even want to put him to death? I have no doubt that Socrates was really <u>annoying</u>. He may be right, that the unexamined life is not worth living. But look around. And look inside your own heart – honestly. Often enough, that unexamined life is the one we choose to lead.

And Socrates is pretty tough on people. Having him engage you in dialogue, leading you to "examine your life," is no walk in the park. He doesn't come right out and say, "What a blithering idiot you are!" No; he's more…civil…than that. But he makes it pretty clear when your beliefs are deeply mistaken. Here's a typical example:

(This is from Plato's dialogue, "Gorgias." The subject is the "big question": What kind of life should one live? Socrates' partner in dialogue is a man named Callicles. He believes that the good life is one of pleasure and satisfying passions. Socrates does not. We'll just eavesdrop on a moment of the dialogue.)

S: Did you say that hunger was pleasant or painful?

C: Painful.

S: And thirst too?

C: Yes, definitely.

S: Do you admit that every deficiency and desire is painful?

C: I do.

S: Very well then. But you say that to drink when you're thirsty is pleasant?

C: Yes.

S: And drinking is a satisfaction of the deficiency and a pleasure?

C: Yes, it is.

S: Then you say that in drinking there is pleasure?

C: Of course.

S: When one is thirsty?

C: Yes.

S: That is, when in pain?

C: Yes.

S: Then do you realize the result? You say a man enjoys pleasure simultaneously with pain. But earlier you said that it is impossible for someone to be faring well and faring ill at the same time.

C: Yes.

S: But you've just agreed it is possible to experience pain at the same time as pleasure.

C: Apparently.

S: Then pleasure is not the same as faring well, nor pain as faring ill, and so the pleasant is different from the good.

C: I do not understand what your quibbles mean, Socrates.

Whew! We can see that dialogue with Socrates is not for the faint of heart. And yet, I want to hold him up tonight as a model of "civility" in its truest sense. True civility, I would claim, is not a matter of "live and let live," or of total relativism (today's "Whatever."). It's not even non-confrontational. Socrates is confrontational; there's no doubt about it. And he's certainly not a total relativist, wary of questioning anyone else's beliefs. But Socrates' mode of engagement with his fellow citizens is a model of civility, in my view, for two reasons:

1) The dialogue is always in the context of seeking a greater good, the good of the whole, the health of the polity, and
2) It is fully respectful of the other person as a fellow citizen.

Socrates' attitude is hardly the brush-off of "Whatever." But it also never descends to personal belittlement or attack.

This, I think, is the civility we crave – and <u>need</u> – in our contemporary context. I brought our attention to Socrates and Aristotle because I think the concept of the "political" as Greek philosophers understood and articulated it is so crucial. The "political," that is, <u>not</u> in the sense of party politics, but rather as an awareness of living in community – an awareness that this is central to our nature as human beings.

In our own American history, these classical precedents and concepts held tremendous sway with the Founding Fathers. Adams, Franklin, Jefferson, Madison, and others – all of these educated men self-consciously saw themselves as founding a new republic on the model of, and informed by, the thinkers of antiquity.

These men read Greek and Roman authors assiduously. In fact, each of them kept what were called "commonplace books" – essentially, notebooks of quotations, in which they copied what they felt were edifying sentiments from the ancients. (Perhaps these jottings were the 18th century equivalent of Twitter?) Thomas Jefferson's correspondence was so thoroughly peppered with quotations from ancient Greek that John Adams exclaimed in exasperation, "Lord! Lord! What can I do with so much Greek?"

Yet, Adams himself spent the summer of 1796, before assuming the American presidency, reading the essays of the Roman statesman and philosopher, Cicero. (A form of preparation for office that might serve our own politicians better than today's hyper-sensitivity to the handlers and the pollsters.) And Adams wrote to his son, John Quincy Adams, "In company with (the Roman authors) Sallust, Cicero, Tacitus, and Livy you will learn Wisdom and Virtue…You will ever remember that all the End of study is to make you a good Man and a useful Citizen."

"A good man (or woman) and a useful citizen" – that, indeed, seems to me the topic before us this evening. "Civility," the quality of being a citizen. For our forefathers, that ability to be a good and useful citizen was intimately bound up with what we could call today "a liberal education." In fact, Jefferson frequently said that, if he had to decide between the classical education his father had provided for him and the estate his father left to him – he would clearly decide in favor of the education. "All the End of study," President John Adams wrote, "is to make you a good Man and a useful Citizen." Education is more valuable than wealth, President Jefferson said. That is certainly not what presidents or governors or congressmen or others have been saying in this country for a long time.

In fact, in recent decades – and with increasing intensity since the economic crisis – all we have heard from policy makers is that the aim of higher education should be wealth and profit, both for individuals and for the country. Most recently, as you know, President Obama has determined that American colleges should be ranked – and it appears that ranking will be based solely on the starting salaries new graduates earn. (Interesting that this idea should be advanced by a college graduate whose first job was community organizer.)

What has happened to the ideal of education for useful and responsible citizenship, for "civility" in its deepest sense? I want to emphasize to you tonight that this value is actually alive and well, flourishing in America's more than 600 small private colleges devoted to liberal learning. But we don't hear much about it. Or – perhaps more accurately – we hear a lot of myths about it that are simply untrue. So, before saying a bit more about the association between liberal arts education and the civility America needs, I want to devote a few minutes to some serious myth-busting.

First, let's be clear about what liberal arts education is and is not. The phrase, "liberal arts" is yet another term from our Latin heritage.

To the Romans, "*artes liberales*," meant the studies appropriate to and necessary for a free human being, as opposed to a slave. [*Liber* here is a different word from the *liber* meaning "book." This one means, "free."] But, today, the historical term, "liberal arts" frequently confuses people, who may think it refers either to liberal politics or to drawing and painting. Neither is true.

Liberal arts is the study of a very broad range of human history, accomplishment, and thought, with an emphasis on developing critical thinking skills, independent judgment, and a taste for lifelong learning. Typically, it includes inquiry in the humanities, social sciences, arts, and sciences. Although this is often misunderstood, liberal arts has always included the natural sciences. And it evolves over time. On today's liberal arts campuses, a student may be studying neuroscience or environmental studies or Arabic, not necessarily the Greek, Latin, and Hebrew that formed the original curriculum. On some campuses, engineering, computer science, or even nursing may be taught in a liberal arts mode – that is, with a greater emphasis on understanding general principles than on memorizing specific data or techniques.

Now, let's get down to the myth-busting. Here are five big ones:

1. Liberal arts education is only for the elite.
2. It's prohibitively expensive to attend a liberal arts college.
3. Graduates have a staggering amount of debt.
4. This kind of education isn't practical.
5. Liberal arts graduates are unemployable.

I would imagine that each of you has heard and read versions of these statements many times over the past few years. You will probably be surprised to learn that none of them is true.

Let me give you some of the facts.

1. <u>Liberal arts education is only for the elite</u>. In fact, private liberal arts colleges enroll about the same or a slightly higher percentage of low-income and under-represented students than do the flagship public universities. Nearly one-third of all private college students are from low income backgrounds. Even more important, all students – but especially under-represented or low-income students – graduate at higher rates and in a shorter amount of time in the liberal arts colleges. (Among Hispanic students who obtained a bachelor's degree, for example, the percentage who graduated in four years at private colleges was nearly twice as high as the percentage who did so within the same amount of time at public colleges).

2. <u>It's prohibitively expensive to attend a liberal arts college</u>. It is true that what liberal arts colleges do – offering small classes, providing close, personal interaction with full-time faculty members, as well as a residential experience – is expensive. But these colleges also offer substantial financial aid to their students. In fact, they offer six times more aid than is provided by the federal government. The result is that, for the average student, the net cost of attendance is very close to that of attending a state school. (And, in the past five years, net tuition and fees at private colleges [adjusted for inflation] have actually decreased by 3.5 percent – another fact that you don't read about in the papers.)

3. <u>Graduates have a staggering amount of debt</u>. How many times in the past 6, 12, 18 months have you read or heard that American student debt is "out of control" – it has topped a trillion dollars! This is one of those moments where a good liberal arts education comes in handy. For basic statistical literacy, you want to know not only the numerator/how much? (in this case, $1 trillion), but the denominator/over how many? The fact is, the number of students attending college in America has grown dramatically in the past decades, from fewer than half of all high school graduates to more than two-thirds. In addition, more students from lower income

families are attending college. Is it surprising, then, that the overall amount of debt has grown? Hardly.

But what about individual students? The term of choice in the press these days seems to be "staggering." Students are graduating with "staggering amounts of debt." The *New York Times* front page story in the summer of 2012, profiling a student who somehow amassed $150,000 of debt for an undergraduate degree, captured public imagination to the extent that many folks seem to believe this is normal. It's not. Let's look at the facts. Overall, less than 3 percent of undergraduates accumulate that level of debt. And their number is overwhelmingly in the for-profit sector (where graduation rates are as low as 22 percent and loan default rates as high as 23 percent).

In America's small, private liberal arts colleges, 28 percent of students graduate with no debt at all. For other graduates, the average amount of debt is about $20,000. The world's most popular car, the Ford Focus, retails today for approximately $16,000-$24,000. Yet, there doesn't seem to be much national hand-wringing over young people incurring "staggering debt" to buy a car. And the automobile depreciates the moment you drive it off the lot. The investment in a college degree appreciates over a lifetime.

Just how much does it appreciate? In a report released recently, the U.S. Census Bureau indicated that lifetime earnings for a college graduate exceed those of non-degree earners by $1 million. A $25,000 investment toward a million-dollar-return seems pretty good. Yet that's not what we are hearing about these days.

4. <u>This kind of education isn't practical</u>. A liberal arts curriculum offers students both broad exposure to a number of different fields of thought (general education) and more in-depth learning in one or more particular methodologies and modes of thought (the major and minor). More often than not these days it includes independent research, under the guidance of a faculty mentor. The emphasis is on being able to form independent judgments, articulate cogent

arguments, and develop the tools and taste for continued, lifelong learning. In a world where we know that our graduates will be employed in roles that don't even exist today, it is hard to see how this kind of learning is not substantially more "practical" than training in a specific skill that may well be obsolete almost upon graduation.

5. <u>Liberal arts graduates are unemployable</u>. First, let's note clearly that the unemployment rate for college graduates, even in the depth of the recession, was about half that for non-college grads. Yet there seems to be a kind of urban mythology that liberal arts grads are only landing jobs as baristas and burger-flippers. Untrue.

You may have seen a recent story in the *New York Times* Sunday magazine highlighting a particularly successful career placement office at a small, private liberal arts college (Wake Forest, NC). Parents there, the reporter noted, were stunned and pleased to hear that 95 percent of graduates were either fully employed or in graduate school within 6 months of graduation. Tucked into the story was the overlooked fact that this statistic is actually comparable for many such colleges.

And yet…how often have you heard the refrain, "What can you do with an English degree?" The answer is: anything. Let me provide just a few examples. These are taken from recent studies of the CEO's of Fortune 500 companies. Michael Eisner of Disney majored in English and Theatre at Denison. The CEO of Procter and Gamble was a French and History major at Hamilton College. Former Secretary of the Treasury, Henry Paulson, majored in English. The CEOs of Corning and of Federated Department Stores both majored in East Asian Studies, one at Earlham College and one at Connecticut College. Harold Varmus, winner of the Nobel Prize in Medicine and one-time head of the National Institutes of Health, majored in English – as did the former CEO of Xerox and Mario Cuomo. Examples like these are legion. At CIC, we are collecting the stories of liberal arts graduates – and what they have done with their educations. Thus far, we have astronauts, entrepreneurs, opera singers, inventors, you name it. Actually, the question is: What *can't* you do with a degree in English, or Philosophy, or French…?

Now, how do the qualities of liberal arts colleges today relate to the issue of civility – and to our friend, Socrates? In several ways, I think. But I want to emphasize in closing one striking connection that might not be immediately apparent. The Greek philosopher, the Founding Fathers, and the American liberal arts college all emphasize the freedom to begin anew, to think differently, to explore fresh ways of being.

In a recent *Wall Street Journal* article entitled, "As Education Declines, So Does Civic Culture," the author laments that, in his view, public education today fails to prepare students for "responsible civic life." He argues this is because – with its emphasis on high-stakes testing and on an indiscriminate relativism (a sort of intellectual "I'm OK; you're OK"), the education system today "discourages finding out what the facts are, revising one's own beliefs on the basis of those facts and being willing to engage with people who don't already agree with you."

But these are precisely the intellectual traits are that are prized and fostered in the environment of the small, residential liberal arts colleges. These very intentional communities provide a society (not unlike Socrates' *polis*), in which young people can learn and practice ways of thinking – in small classes and seminars focused on discussion, in close dialogue with adult mentors, in the responsibility they must take for building relationships with others who differ from them – that develop their capacity for citizenship, for civility.

In fact, I will go further and say that liberal arts education importantly develops not only ways of <u>thinking</u>, but ways of <u>being</u> that matter to the civil society we'd like to see. In a thought-provoking book published by Princeton, *The Importance of Being Civil:*

the Struggle for Political Decency, sociologist Jonathan Hall suggests that "A civil society will allow the individual room to experiment." It is one "in which individuals have at least the chance of trying to create their own selves."

Interestingly, Socratic dialogue also encourages this kind of experimentation. Time and time again, Socrates will invite his interlocutor to re-think his positions, to try another tack, to set out on a fresh path in their mutual efforts to arrive at truths. Socratic dialogues are punctuated with remarks like, "It seems, then, we must attack the question in another way." "Apparently we must begin all over again," "Perhaps we must approach what we are looking for in another way." In other words, in their joint search for understanding, Socrates invites his fellow citizens to experiment, to be flexible, not to get "stuck" in an ideological position. Wouldn't this be a refreshing form of civility?

This kind of exploration, experimenting with differing ideas, possibilities, different "selves" if you will, has been a unique strength of American liberal arts education. Unlike other nations, we have not "tracked" our youth, marking them from an early age as university-bound or not, scientists or lawyers, tradesmen or teachers. The examples of liberal arts graduates I cited earlier illustrate the range of possibilities our system enables young people to explore.

In one of the very best books to have come out in recent years on education, Andrew Delbanco's *College: What It Was, Is, and Should Be,* this Columbia-based scholar cites the words he found in the manuscript diary of a student at a small, Methodist college in Virginia in the 1850's as perhaps the best formulation of what college (and, I would add, what an education for true citizenship and civility) should be: "Oh that the Lord would show me," this young man wrote, "how to think and how to choose."

On a very similar note, from our own century, I find especially inspiring words that my friend, Richard Brodhead, delivered in an opening address to the freshmen at Yale.

"You have come to one of the great fresh starts in your life," he said, "one of the few chances your life will offer to step away from the person you've been taken for and decide anew what you would like to become....Far be it from me to say what exemplary life you should propose for yourself, but I implore you not to miss this opportunity to chart one."

To me, this thought encapsulates that ideal of openness, of possibility, of grander aspirations that I would hope mark both our American education system and its capacity to foster a truly civil society.

James Cuno

On

Civility and the Museum

J Paul Getty once said, "In my opinion, an individual without any love of the arts cannot be considered completely civilized."

The J. Paul Getty Trust's commitment to a civil society is front and center in our Mission Statement, which says, in part, that the Getty is committed to "the presentation, preservation, and dissemination of new knowledge about the world's artistic legacy…with the conviction that a greater and more profound sensitivity to and knowledge of the visual arts and their many histories is crucial to the promotion of a vital and civil society".

In the era of the Enlightenment, the term "civil" was applied to society as distinguished from the state or the political realm. In this it referred to the Roman law idea of *civitas*, or the idea of voluntary relations among persons that was thus neither narrowly familial nor formally constituted by the state. Emphasis here was on "voluntary": individuals coming together outside of formal bonds policed by the state or, later, by the church. A distinct sphere of human activity, "civil society" was the product of individuals gathering together – physically or virtually – to address each other openly in coffee house conversations and debates and in the rapidly rising print media of newspapers and journals. Substantiated by developing social contract and natural law theories, this led to the legitimacy of the radical idea that society preceded government, that it was self-organizing, and that the legitimacy of government depended on its serving the needs of the people.

Public art museums date from this same period. The British Museum, for example, was founded in 1753, the result of a bequest to the nation – importantly to the *nation* and not to the *Crown* – and was governed by Trustees for the benefit "not only for the Inspection and Entertainment of the learned and the curious, but for the general Use and Benefit of the Public." It was a secular, disputatious space where facts about the world – then, all manner of natural and artificial things, but now, with the disciplinary division between art and natural history, all kinds of works of art – could be subjected to rigorous, scientific analysis with the promise that this would produce truths about the world which themselves would be subjected to analyses, constantly refined, discarded, or confirmed. The authority to critique things and resulting truths was not limited to specialists, but was available to everyone whose intelligence could be cultivated by access to clearly articulated and argued philosophical positions. This was a cardinal principle of the Enlightenment: clear thinking, plain words, candor, and modesty shared among a "commonwealth of polite letters," a community of individuals across political borders united by a common curiosity about the world.

I have written about the importance of encyclopedic museums as cosmopolitan institutions dedicated to the proposition that by gathering and presenting representative examples of the world's diverse artistic cultures "under one roof," they work to dissipate ignorance and superstition about the world and promote tolerance of difference as a condition of the world, encouraging identification with others as a shared sense of being human, of having in every meaningful way a common history with a common future at stake.

In this, encyclopedic museums are crucial to the formation of a civil society and the promotion of the common good. And in the age in which we live, when resurgent nationalism, sectarian violence, and military-backed, hardened ideological conflict prosper unabated, encyclopedic museums matter, now more than ever.

Increasingly, encyclopedic museums are being criticized as instruments of the state and of empire, sites of symbolic transactions that confirm the power of the state and the hegemony of the elite over the will of the individual. I argue the opposite. I argue that by presenting the artifacts of one time and culture next to those of other times and cultures without privilege or prejudice, encyclopedic museums are dedicated to the dissemination of learning as a force for understanding, tolerance, and the dissipation of ignorance and superstition, and are arguments against an essentialized, state-derived cultural identity in favor of a cosmopolitan one, one that acknowledges and demonstrates the truth about art – that it has never known political boundaries but has always been dynamic and hybrid, formed through contact and exchange with diverse peoples.

In the globalized, polyglot, multiethnic world in which we daily confront our many differences, understanding and tolerance of difference is foundational to any notion of civility. And civility is essential to resolving differences in our world: personal or political, local or international. One need only Google the term to find sites for "Civility in Public Discourse," the "National Civility Center," "The Civility Project," "The Institute for Civility in Government," and hundreds more. And with the campaign for the U.S. presidency in full swing, calls for civility – an acts of *incivility* – are common currency.

But not just here; everywhere. The collapse of empires and the rise of globalism that have brought different people into contact with one another in unprecedented numbers both within and across or national borders) is unprecedented. This has strained the nation-state and changed the way we think of nations: no longer as politically defined and territorially circumscribed, but as discursive fields of cultural signification.

It has led the Indian-born, New York-based social theorist Arjun Appadurai to argue that the principles and procedures of the modern nation-state – "the idea of a sovereign and stable territory, the idea of a containable and countable population, the idea of a reliable census, and the idea of stable and transparent categories" – have come so unglued in our era that they have produced "new incentives for cultural purification as more nations lose the illusion of national economic sovereignty or well being." The result, he claims, is a dangerous, often violent "narcissism of minor differences."

"The map of the world," the late cultural critique Edward Said once wrote, "has no divinely or dogmatically sanctioned spaces, essences, or privileges. However, we can speak of secular space, and of humanly constructed and interdependent histories that are fundamentally knowable…" Such a space and such histories are reliably only created by individuals in civil discourse with one another. The only alternatives are tyranny and chaos.

When I wrote my most recent book about the encyclopedic museum, I was the director of the Art Institute of Chicago, which, in all modesty, is one of the world's great encyclopedic museums in one of the world's great cities. Since then, I have become President and CEO of the J. Paul Getty Trust, which comprises not only a museum, but the Getty Conservation Institute, Getty Research Institute, and the Foundation. Through its exhibitions, conservation, research and grant-making, the Getty has a truly global reach, advancing research, conservation, and presentation of the visual arts and cultural heritage in Los Angeles and on all seven continents, from the dawn of time to the present day.

The Getty has consulted on the preservation of traces of hominids in Tanzania 3.7 million years ago, helped conserve and exhibit ancient icons from the Sinai, saved the archives and rewritten the history of post-war Los Angeles artists, and is currently working to preserve Roman mosaics throughout the eastern Mediterranean and, in Egypt, King Tut's tomb.

We are leading research into the conservation of modern materials in contemporary art, and in cutting-edge lighting strategies for museums to reduce the damage done to artwork by exposure to excessive levels of light. We are making grants to strengthen the museum infrastructure in Africa, to develop museum leadership all over the world, connect art histories and digitize collections and research materials to make them universally available. And in doing so, we are pursuing are primary mission: supporting the visual arts in the promotion of a vital and civil society, not only by preserving and promoting the visual arts but by partnering with individuals across political borders and building capacity among museum, academic, and conservation professionals.

Closer to home, the Getty is using the visual arts to promote civility within LA's schools. The U.S. Department of Education recently announced finding from a study on Arts Education in Public Elementary and Secondary Schools that nearly 4 million students receive no specific instruction in the visual arts. This report also found that the nation's poorest students, the ones who could benefit the most from arts education, are receiving it the least.

A new NEA Research Report on **Arts and Achievement in At-Risk Youth** found that teenagers and young adults of low socioeconomic status who have a history of in-depth arts involvement show better academic outcomes. They earn better grades and have higher rates of college enrollment and attainment. They have higher career goals and they are more civically engaged. Young adults who had intensive arts experiences in high school are more likely to show civic-minded behavior, with comparatively high levels of volunteering, voting and engagement with local or school politics.

According to the National Arts Education Association: "Facilitated learning experiences with works of art cultivate global perspectives and an appreciation of the diversity of cultures, ideas, and human experiences. The study of works of art promotes the development of creative and critical thinking skills that are important to success in life as well as in school. These include inquiry, analysis, and interpretation as well as flexibility, imagination, and reflection."

For all these reasons, the Getty works in close partnership with the Los Angeles Unified School District to provide arts experiences at the Getty and in the classroom, particularly for students in Title One Schools.

The importance of art as a critical element in the creation of a civil society will not diminish, indeed with the introduction of digital technology its importance will only increase as access to the visual arts and the history of art become widespread on a global basis. The Getty is playing a role in this effort as well, having recently launched a global digital portal to provide scholars, researchers, and the general public eventual access to all books of art history published prior to 1923 and in the leading museum and university libraries in Europe and North America (soon enough this will be expanded to libraries in South America and Asia). At the same time, we are constantly populating on our Web-site with new information about works of art in our Museum's collection, as well as the latest discoveries of our conservation scientists and new and increasingly enriched curricular materials and study aids for teachers anywhere in the world.

A recent digital project is in the service of our colleagues in the Middle East, who are charged with the protection of and research into the world's archaeological heritage within their national borders. Called Middle Eastern Geodatabase for Antiquities-Jordan, or

MEGA-J, it is a bilingual Arabic-English, Web-based national geographic information system for Jordan's Department of Antiquities that will serve as the primary tool for the Department of Antiquities in its ongoing work to inventory, monitor, and manage Jordan's vast number of archaeological sites. Launched in partnership with the World Monuments Fund, MEGA-J's software is low-cost, open-source, non-proprietary, and has wide compatibility with similar systems of Jordanian national and local authorities. To date its success is such that the site is richly populated with information – photographic and verbally descriptive – entered by our Jordanian colleagues according to their needs and interests. And it is beginning to be adopted by Iraqi and other antiquities authorities in the region.

We are currently expanding the basic premise of MEGA-J to the larger universe of all manner of post-archaeological immoveable heritage, including buildings and other structures, cultural landscapes, heritage ensembles and districts around the world. Called ARCHES, a system supporting heritage inventory and management, the project is still in development and, like MEGA-J, will employ open source software and open data encoding standards, and will be populated by its users to their needs and interests.

Let me conclude by bringing us back to basics: to the foundation of civility as experienced in art museums. Civility requires that we seek to understand the concerns of others, that we learn to respect that others have views and experiences different from our own. To achieve this, we need to put ourselves aside for the moment, our personal interests and preoccupations. The 19th-century poet and critic Matthew Arnold described literary criticism as the effort "to see the object as in itself it really is." The mid-20th century literary critic Lionel Trilling concurred. He wrote:

"The object, whether it be a phenomenon of nature, or a work of art, or an idea or a system of ideas, or a social problem, or indeed, a person, is not to be seen as it, or he or she, appears to our habitual thought, to our predilections and prejudices, to our casual or hasty inspection, but as it really is *in itself*, in its own terms, in these alone. Objectivity, we might say, is the respect we give to the object, as it exists apart from us."

This is what the Enlightenment founders of the encyclopedic museum meant by rigorous, scientific analysis: to suspect all received opinion and unverifiable truths and, instead, to subject them – and the data on which they are based – to critique as *in themselves they really are*, and then to critique one's conclusions on the same terms.

To do this, as Trilling reminded us, we have to respect the object – in the case of art museums, a work of art – "as it exists apart from us," the thing there before us, that is not us and that does not conform to our habitual thought or predilections, but that preceded our seeing it, that existed apart from us, and that requires our putting ourselves aside to come to grips with it in all its stubborn matter-of-factness as in itself it really is.

The 20th-century French mystical philosopher Simone Weil wrote of this on similar terms. At the moment we see something beautiful, she wrote, we "give up our imaginary position at the center…A transformation then takes place at the very roots of our sensibility, in our immediate reception of sense impressions and psychological impressions." And we experience the moral benefits of stepping aside in favor of something else, of acknowledging that something exists on terms with which we have to come to grips, to understand and appreciate it as it is, different from us. The English moral philosopher Iris Murdoch wrote of this moment that "anything which alters consciousness in the direction of unselfishness, objectivity and realism is to be connected with virtue."

To experience beauty, therefore – and this is the principal experience that one can have in art museums – and in encyclopedic museums, different kinds of beauties in a variety of different and unfamiliar works of art from distant times and places – is to experience an "unselfing," and all the energy one formerly put into the service of protecting, guarding, and advancing the self is then free to be put in the service of another.

This is the promise of encyclopedic museums, and why they matter now more than ever. They illicit an objective response in us, encouraging us to set ourselves aside to see the works of others as in themselves they really are; and then to realize that in this, they are like us and the objects with which we more easily identify. And then, as the philosopher Paul Ricoeur has written, "When we discover that there are several cultures instead of just one and consequently at the time when we acknowledge the end of a sort of cultural monopoly, be it illusory or real, we are threatened with destruction by our own discovery. Suddenly it becomes possible that there are just others, that we ourselves are an 'other' among others."

And this is the basis of civility: the respect for the other, and then others with others in a common pursuit of understanding. And it is why I hold that the art museum and cosmopolite cultural institutions like the J. Paul Getty Trust play a vital role in developing and strengthen civil society, and why they matter today, now perhaps more than ever.

William Bratton

On

Civility and Law Enforcement

What I want to talk with you about is the profession that I've committed most of my adult life to, and that's the profession of law enforcement. It's profession that I have the utmost pride in. It's a profession that has profound impact in our democracy and our democratic society and I have a mantra that I use in policing and it's that cops count, police matter – and particularly in a democracy, where we are the guardians of the rights and privileges that are promised by our democracy.

We are privileged and fortunate in this country to live in one of the oldest and arguably the most successful experiments that has ever been undertaken to implement democracy.

I want to share with you the foundations of our democracy that begin with our Declaration of Independence, our Constitution – certainly every president has espoused lines in support of it, whether it's Lincoln in his Gettysburg Address or Franklin Roosevelt in Freedom from Fear and his remarks in the midst of the Depression in the '30s. That it is a platform on which all of our principles are built. And it might pay sometimes to be reminded of our foundations.

The foundation of our democracy, in terms of its success, is a civility that it ensures and requires and that is, fortunately, practiced by most of our citizens.

In his book, *Civility in America*, Joshua Levenberg writes in the forward, "All of civility depends on being able to contain the rage of individuals."

Joe Rosenthal, in the same book, in his essay writes, "Civility is a core principle of public life. Civility offers a better way of life." And, "In the midst of tough circumstances, we treat individuals with dignity and respect."

In our Constitution: "We the people of the United States, in order to form a more perfect union, establish justice and ensure domestic tranquility." The first and foremost promise of our government is domestic tranquility, which is basically freedom and respect for our freedom and respect for our laws.

In our Declaration of Independence, "When in the Course of human events it becomes necessary for one people to dissolve the political bands which have connected them with another and to assume among the powers of the earth, the separate and equal station to which the Laws of Nature and of Nature's God entitled them, a decent respect to the opinions of mankind requires that they should declare the causes which impel them to the separation."

So our founding fathers based their Revolution, their rebellion, on the issue that they and their colleagues in this country, the colonies, had been disrespected by the King. "We hold these truths to be self-evident, that all men are created equal, that they are endowed by their Creator with certain unalienable Rights, that among these are Life, Liberty and the pursuit of Happiness. – That to secure these rights, Governments are instituted among men, deriving their just powers from the consent of the governed." Civility, consent, respect.

In terms of George Washington, our founding father, George was obviously thinking about the issues of respect and civility long before he led the Revolution.

When he was 16 years old, one of his exercises was transcribing the "Rules of Civility and Decent Behaviour in Company and Conversation," about 125 of these. It's written in very quaint and old English, and gives you a taste of what George was thinking about when he was thinking about civility and respect.

1: Every action done in Company, ought to be with Some Sign of Respect, to those that are Present – number 1, respect.

2: When in Company, put not your Hands to any Part of the Body, not usually Discovered.

3: Shew Nothing to your Friend(sic) that may affright him.

4: In the Presence of Others Sing not to yourself with a humming Noise, nor Drum with your Fingers or Feet.

5: If You Cough, Sneeze, Sigh, or Yawn, do it not Loud but Privately; and Speak not in your Yawning, but put Your handkerchief(sic) or Hand before your face and turn aside.

6: Sleep not when others speak.

7. Sit not when others stand. Speak not when you should hold your peace, walk not on when others shop and put not off your clothes in the presence of others nor go out of your chambers half-dressed.

There are 125 of these, so George Washington was spending a lot of time thinking about the issue of respect for others and their space.

In my profession, the profession I'm so proud of, our foundation really began with the British. In the 1840s, under Sir Robert Peel as Home Secretary, the British were creating, for the first time, an organized policing force in the city of London. There was a real aversion to the idea of a uniformed police force, and they were met with great resistance when they were first formed.

So Robert Peel understood clearly that to win general acceptance, the police, the bobby, the British bobby, the predecessor of every American police officer, was going to have to perform to a list of standards, if you will, to a level.

And first and foremost of those rules, Peel's Nine Principles of Policing, were going to be the issue, if you will, of respect.

And I'd like to read just three of the nine. These are principles that I've been observing since I was first exposed to them when I came into policing in the 1970s.

1. The basic mission for which the police exist is to prevent crime and disorder.

2. The ability of the police to perform their duties is dependent upon public approval of police actions.

7. Police, at all times, should maintain a relationship with the public that gives reality to the historic tradition that the police are the public and the public are the police, the police being the only members of the public who are paid to give full-time attention to duties which are incumbent on every citizen in the interest of community welfare and existence.

In our democracy, police exist, quite simply, to control behavior. We are given extraordinary powers to do that. We are about the only entity in our government that is authorized to take a life in the performance of our duty. We are authorized to stop, to question, to detain, to frisk, to arrest, to use force, when necessary to overcome resistance – extraordinary, awesome powers.

The powers that are given to us are really those that society has agreed upon in our democracy, that, in exchange for the freedom that is promised in our Declaration, our Constitution, in our various ordinances and our laws. We are expected, for the common good, to respect the law, to respect each other in our adherence of the law, but also to respect the freedom that is guaranteed to protest, the freedom to have a different opinion, the freedom to be different.

At all times it is expected that we respect the law, that we obey it, that we adhere to it, that, if we violate it, it is understood that it is with consequence and that the willful violation will be met with a certain degree of punishment, whether it's for civil disobedience or for the action or commission of a criminal offense or behavior.

In our society, we entrust the police with the awesome powers to control and regulate behavior. There's an expression used in policing, one of the first I remember from my training as a recruit in 1970 in the Boston Police Department, "The public deserves respect. The police must earn it."

The public deserves respect. They are guaranteed respect by the law. The police are not guaranteed that. They must earn it by their behavior.

Sir Robert Peel's Nine Principles

Policing in this country, going back certainly to the 1700s, to the 1800s and on up into the 1960s, and finally 1970, when I entered policing, had a very checkered history, to put it mildly. We were instruments of government, as we remain today. In the United States, we report to political leadership, we report to civilian leadership, unlike in some countries. And the responsibility of the police is to be responsive to that political leadership, to the laws that we are expected to enforce, to the rules and the ordinances.

And, unfortunately, even in our democracy, as we have grown, as we have matured, as we have wrestled with the issues of the day, over the years, over the centuries, that police have oftentimes found themselves, looking back, in many respects, as oppressors, found themselves effectively enforcing laws that, in today's society, are seen to be truly unfair, unnecessary, certainly not respectful of many of our citizens.

Growing up through the 1800s, even as Sir Robert Peel is founding modern policing in the 1840s, police oftentimes were employed, particularly regarding the labor movement in the late 1800s and early 1900s, to act as strike-breakers on behalf of businesses who were beholden to political leadership, or political leadership that was beholden to the business community. We were often required to enforce unpopular laws, Prohibition being one. During the '20s and moving slowly into the '30s, widespread disobedience of that national law found the police in the middle, enforcing it or not enforcing it amid the incredible corruption and brutality and disrespect that they engaged in and employed during that particularly troublesome period of time.

Into the '40s and '50s, police increasingly, in city after city after city, lost their way, even as political leadership, in many of those cities, lost its way, in the sense that it became corrupt, it became brutal, it became incompetent, it became insensitive and, in many parts of the country, enforced segregation laws. In many parts of the country, police were involved in desegregation, involved in ways in which their behavior was oftentimes questioned.

Policing has always had a difficult task – to enforce the law – but the challenge for the police is always, in that enforcing, to not break the law, in that enforcing to be respectful, civil, in that enforcing to be consistent. And we were not.

We were none of those things throughout the country, to the extent that in the beginning of the 1960s, at the Supreme Court level, at the national political level, and increasingly, at the local level, additional controls were put on the police because it was felt that we were beginning to not be respectful of the law.

Police were found to not be respectful of many of our citizens, particularly citizens of color, citizens who were poor, citizens who were different. We were found to be, in many of our practices, brutal. We were found to be, in our enforcement of law, inconsistent, oftentimes because of corruption.

The state of policing in the '50s and 1960s was something that was crying out for change – crying out for change because the respect that we would expect to have because of our particular role, our particular place in society, we didn't have it.

And why? You get what you give, and we were not giving respect.

We were giving disrespect. We were giving brutality. We were giving corruption, not everywhere but enough so that the Supreme Court in the 1960s began, through a series of rulings, to begin to control the behavior of the police, the Miranda warning, the fact that police were consistently violating the rights, the civil rights, the civil liberties of many of the suspects they were dealing with.

The Escobedo decision, the Exclusionary Rule – police were found to be consistently violating the rules of the Constitution, and thus their behavior needed to be more controlled.

Additionally, our society in the 1960s was going through a time of incredible turmoil, when it appeared that civility was, in fact, a thing of the past, that whether it was the demonstrations against the segregation – the Civil Rights Movement – the demonstrations against the Vietnam War, the demonstrations against a society that was thought to be too controlling.

We were literally spinning out of control for a significant part of that decade, some of it well intended, in terms of the changes that were being sought. It was a consistent and intensive effort to effectively loosen up, if you will, on the controls that society was placing on the behavior of many people who didn't want any controls on their lives.

As we come out of the 1960s into the '70s, it was a time of profound, meaningful, progressive change in American policing. We had been found deficient. I joined the Boston Police Department in 1970, and I entered a department that was going through the last stages of that era. It was a brutal department. It was a corrupt department. It was a racist department. It certainly was not respectful of its members.

The leadership and their treatment of the rank and file was so disrespectful of the rights of the officers that the union movement was born in policing, and I believe one of the first and strongest police unions in the United States was in the City of Boston.

And, indeed, I got my first job in Boston because of that union winning a labor contract that required there be two police officers in every car, because the dangerous situations in the street warranted not having just one officer in the car. I benefitted by that union movement, which was really about respect and the lack of respect that the officers of that time received.

But as I entered the Boston Police Department, the last vestiges of it were still there, so much so that by 1972 I was ready to leave the department. I just didn't feel that this was the profession that I thought it was going to be, and certainly that the Boston police were not what I thought policing was all about.

But fortunately, fortunately, a man of vision, a leader, came into the Boston Police Department, Bob DiGrazia, the first outside Commissioner in a long time. And he came in with new ideas.

He came in with a vision of what policing should be. He came in with a vision of police as honest. He came in with a vision of police as professional. He came in with a vision of police as being servants of the people, people who were required to earn respect, while giving it.

And he changed that department and he became the model for me for the rest of my career, in the six subsequent police departments I was privileged to lead and the many others I have consulted with. And part of the movement he was beginning to lead was the movement toward professionalism.

And the professional movement in policing, first and foremost, was built around the idea that as professionals, you needed to respect the law that we were empowered to enforce, respect the public for whom we worked, and respect for each other, a sergeant for his police officers, a lieutenant for his squad, a police chief for the men and women of his department.

And I saw my profession change significantly in the '70s and '80s, even as we were facing the social turmoil that, coming out of the '60s, continued to explode into the '80s, in particular, as the issue of drug use, as the issue of violence, particularly shaped by increasing exposure and acquisition of increasingly more powerful firearms, took a phenomenal toll on our society, and our civilities began to lessen dramatically. And the conditions on our streets changed dramatically.

We saw it everywhere, disrespect for public property, graffiti everywhere, disrespect for each other's rights, if you will, and the way people accosted each other on the streets, aggressive begging, squeegee pests, prostitution, that we were a society that, in many respects, was starting to lose our way, the acceptance of violence that the Mayor referenced in his remarks, the idea that some behaviors should be excused away because of the condition of people.

And we were in tough shape in the 1980s. And the professional model of policing was not responsive to that change. It was failing. As crime rates were going up, respect for police was declining because we were not effective in protecting and serving and guiding.

But then a new movement began. In the late '80s, I was privileged to be part of it, and many officers were also. And that was community policing. Community policing saved American policing, and I would argue that it saved America, at least saved the cities of America, in that it brought back the idea that police are a part of society. They can't be the thin blue line standing over there and the public over here. Going back to Sir Robert Peel's statement, "We are the police and the police are us."

And that's what we returned to in the 1990s with community policing. It was based on three foundation pillars: partnership/collaboration, problem solving and prevention. We had moved away from the idea of preventing crime – and disorder and incivility – and allowed ourselves to be only responding to it.

Police were created to prevent crime – Sir Robert Peel's first principle, to prevent crime, to prevent incivility by our presence, by our demeanor.

And in the 1990s, we began to do that. We began, in city after city: Boston, my first experience; New York, secondly with the Transit Police; back to Boston again; then New York and more recently in L.A. I've watched my profession return to its roots, and those roots are based on the foundation of our democracy, on the foundation of our professional police philosophy of community policing.

And community policing is all about respect, partnership where the police respect the community to the extent that we want to partner with the community to prioritize the problems that the community wants us to address with them. If it's incivility, if it's serious crime, if it's whatever the issue that's creating fear or disorder in their community, we, the police, agree that we will work in collaboration. We will respect the will of the people for what they want prioritized.

It's also about this idea of prevention, that in the '60s, '70s and '80s, we began to excuse away a lot of behavior, for a lot of reasons, and that was a mistake. We began to excuse away the incivilities. We began to excuse away the abhorrent behavior. In some respects, we began to excuse away, even, some of the crimes.

In the 90s, we began to refocus, once again, and police helped lead that way – certainly in New York City because of its particular position in our country, the largest city, and its worldwide status. Changes there in the '70s and '80s were so profound that the country had an image of New York, the world had an image of New York, as a place that was going down for the count and was not likely to come back.

Mario Cuomo, the governor in 1989, was asked about conditions in New York City at the time he was thinking about running for president, a time when there were 2,200 murders in the city, 7,000 people shot and the streets of the city looked like Dante's Inferno. The whole place had gone to hell. His comment was, "Maybe this is as good as it gets."

Well, when political leadership abrogates the responsibility to maintain civility in the streets, in the subways and in the parks and in the schools, then we're abrogating and giving up on democracy, because that's what democracy promises, freedom, but freedom within limits.

And what police are expected to do is operate within those limits: You can't break the law to enforce it. You can't discriminate. You can't be disrespectful, because you get what you give.

And so, much of the racial tension in this country, so much of the tension between rich and poor, so much of the class issue, is as a result of police actions over the years, at the behest of political leadership, government, laws that we have now seen to be truly and incredibly unjust when we look back at conditions, whether it be slavery in the 17 and 1800s, whether we look at issues around the Civil Rights Movement, women's suffrage, where the police were effectively the instruments of government to oppress.

We are changing, and we are changing for the better. And law enforcement can lead the way – law enforcement, because we are so present in our society, with our blue uniforms, with the powers that we have. As the police go, I would argue, so goes society.

When police in the 1990s began, as part of the "broken windows theory," take care of the little things, it helped create a situation where the big problems don't develop. And the little things were like graffiti, the idea that we weren't going to tolerate that anymore; the aggressive begging; the street disturbances and the squeegee person in New York City; the prostitution and the street narcotic sales. But, in all things, to be successful, we had to do it respectfully. We had to do it in a civil manner.

Today in this country we are engaged in a great debate, and it's going to be very interesting to watch where it goes in the next few years. That great debate is around the issue of police powers to stop, question and frisk.

"Stop-and-Frisk" is the term most commonly used. They always leave out the most important part, which is why are police stopping a person in the first place, because they have reasonable suspicion that a crime has been, is or is about to be, committed by the individual that they are stopping. And what are they stopping that person for? To question, and if, in the course of that questioning or because of actions they may have observed, they feel that that person might be armed in such a way to cause harm to themselves, the police, or to innocent bystanders, they are authorized by law to frisk.

It is the most basic tool of American policing. It was upheld constitutionally with *Terry v. Ohio* in the 1960s. I can guarantee for you that there is going to be a push in the next few years to try and attack *Terry v. Ohio* and attack those powers of the police. And that's at great risk to our society, because, without that tool, police would be like a doctor asked to work without anesthesia or without so many of the prescriptions that can be used to make you well.

The obligation on behalf of the police is to, while practicing stop, question and frisk, is to employ the fourth leg of that four-legged stool - because it is a four-legged stool. The fourth leg is to do it with respect, within the law, respectfully, consistently.

So whether you're stopping a white person, a black person, a man, a woman, a juvenile, an adult, you do it in such a way that as the experience ends, if you've done it correctly, the person understands why you stopped them and doesn't feel that they were inappropriately violated by being disrespectfully treated.

And so, as policing goes forward into the 21st century, that issue is going to be first and foremost, in terms of ensuring that the training of police, the supervision of police, the leadership of police, is working on that issue. It is the basic foundation of policing and it's a tool that we cannot afford to lose, because if we lose it, then you lose it. And if we lose it, it will be because we were doing it disrespectfully.

I would like to close with a reflection of who I am. And who I am in policing in the public sector is an optimist. I am an eternally optimistic person about my profession. Even when I entered it in the

1970s and as bad as it was, I was optimistic that I could find someplace where it was not like that. But fortunately, I didn't have to go searching elsewhere, because a new leader came in and made a change.

Bob Dilenschneider is also an optimist. In this book that he caused to be published about civility, there's an article by him with his comment, "With so many people of good heart and mind focusing on our crises of incivility in public life, however, it is my hope and belief, as it is several of the book's contributors, that if there is a theme throughout the book, it is this idea of hope and optimism that, if it gets bad, that it can get better." And he closes that, "Within the next decade, we begin to see a change for the positive."

As I look at American policing in this next decade, if we can meet the challenges of Stop-and-Frisk, of racial insensitivity, of allegations of corruption and brutality, and meet them in a transparent way, where we are willing to be evaluated, where we are willing to partner up with communities in a transparent, productive way, then the next decade will be a better decade than the one we are living in and the one we lived in in the 1990s.

The 1990s weren't too bad. After 25 years of steady crime increase in the United States, in the 1990s it began to go down. Violent crime went down over 40 percent, serious crime – burglaries, car thefts – went down by 30 percent, and in cities like New York, down by 70 or 80 percent. In Los Angeles over the last ten years it's down almost 60 percent.

So, even as we moved into the first decade of the 21st century, the residual benefits of the investment we made in the 1990s were still holding fast in the midst of the worst economy that we had seen since the Great Depression.

And, as we now move into the second decade of that 21st century, there is optimism, despite the significant cutbacks in police staffing and resources, because we've gotten better.

We learn from the past. We're shaped by the past and, as we go forward, we have returned to our roots that Sir Robert Peel described for us, that we are of the people. And the people are us and we are them, and we are truly partnered up with them. And being partnered up with each other, we can accomplish so much more.

Thomas J. Donohue

On

Civility in Free Speech and Free Enterprise

Mahatma Gandhi once advised us to "be the change that you wish to see in the world." In other words, if you want to begin to solve a problem, start by looking in the mirror. Each of us has a personal responsibility to ensure that we practice what we preach.

At the U.S. Chamber of Commerce, we're in a pretty rough-and-tumble business. We lobby governments in Washington and around the world. We represent business in the courts of law, before the regulatory agencies, in the press, and in the court of public opinion.

We work to hammer out common positions and principles among 3 million very diverse companies, state and local chambers, and industry groups. That's probably the hardest part of my job. We vigorously defend the free enterprise system at a very challenging time. And we do all of this in the face of criticism and attacks from some pretty serious and worthy adversaries.

It's not for the faint of heart. But one thing I always tell our members and our employees – especially new employees – is that no matter how tough the battles or how big the responsibilities, don't forget the rules of engagement at the Chamber.

They're pretty simple. Conduct yourself with high integrity and good manners – and after that, it's a barroom brawl! Well, I'm sort of joking about the barroom brawl. But I'm damn serious about integrity and good manners. We simply won't tolerate rude, unfriendly, or disrespectful behavior in our workplace or among those we deal with, including our adversaries.

The way I put it is this: You can be tough without being a jerk.

I also encourage our folks at the Chamber to be open to different ideas and alternative opinions. Don't just talk to those with whom you already agree. My approach is I'll meet with almost anyone and talk to almost anybody, including those who are well known for their anti-business views.

Sometimes I'm asked why are you wasting your time. Well, more often than not, it's not a waste of time. I usually come away having learned something. Occasionally, you can establish a certain respect and rapport even while continuing to disagree, which can lead to solutions later on. You can pick up a new insight and perhaps challenge one of your own assumptions. The worst that happens is that by better understanding *their* arguments, you can strengthen your own.

That's how we try to conduct ourselves at the Chamber. Lord knows we are far from perfect. But like I said, restoring civility is something we *all* need to take personally and work on every day.

Factors Undermining Civility

So what are some of the factors that seem to be making America a less civil society? I'm not a social scientist, but I've been around a while, I've interacted with a lot of people, and I've witnessed a lot of history.

I think it's clear that tough economic times can make us less civil. Alternatively, there's nothing like a booming economy to make most people feel good and play nice.

It sure helps in government, too. Go talk to the folks in North Dakota, where their coffers are overflowing thanks to the energy boom. Ask them whether the debates over surpluses are more civil than the debates they used to have over deficits. I think you can guess the answer!

But when citizens and governments must share in scarcity, when jobs are few, when opportunities are limited, and when families are struggling economically, divisions and rancor in our communities come to the fore. Resentment, anger and envy grow.

We've made some improvements in our economic circumstances since the crisis of 2008. But the fact is we are stuck in the weakest and slowest economic recovery since World War II. Under such conditions, it's part of human nature to blame someone else for difficult conditions. Many are looking for scapegoats, and regrettably, some of our politicians are all too willing to oblige by engaging in the cheap rhetoric of class warfare.

As I'll discuss later on, revving up the engines of American growth and prosperity, and making sure the benefits are broadly shared, can go a long way to restoring a more cooperative, tolerant and respectful society.

Change and uncertainty can also contribute to incivility – especially as we grapple with the new realities of globalization and America's changing demographics.

Americans have historically handled change and uncertainty better than most. But in modern times, change and uncertainty can quickly add up to fear and insecurity. And this fear and insecurity can trigger less civil and less tolerant behavior toward one another and toward those who may be different.

Right now we're trying to get a potentially historic immigration reform bill through the Congress to the president's desk. We must do this for the sake of our economy, our security, and our legacy as an open and welcoming nation.

While there may be many viewpoints in this debate, everyone can agree that the current system is completely broken.

As the immigration debate has unfolded, so far I have been pleased and relieved by the relative lack of recrimination directed at "those people" – the immigrants who have come here, some illegally, in search of a better life for themselves and their children.

There are legitimate questions to debate about the proper course to take on immigration. Most participants in this debate are doing so on the merits and in good faith. But there can be no excuse for lashing out at "those people," because guess what, virtually all of us are – or once were – "those people."

The aging of our society is another unstoppable demographic reality and a somewhat fearsome change that could undermine our unity and erode civility.

Ten thousand baby boomers are turning 65 every day and will do so for the next 17 years. Almost every one of them – rich, poor or somewhere in between – is expecting to be supported by our massive entitlement programs, namely Social Security, Medicare and Medicaid.

The Chamber is leading the fight for entitlement reform – common-sense modifications acted upon now in order to avoid much greater pain later on. The economics alone are compelling enough – these programs are already consuming all the money the federal government now collects in income taxes. Before too long they will squeeze out spending for all other national priorities.

But more than economics is at stake. So is our cohesion as a society. America cannot afford the kind of intergenerational conflict that will inevitably occur if we continue to force a massive transfer of wealth from the young to the old.

I believe that our country's failings in the arena of public education have also contributed to a more divided and less civil society. There's a lot of focus on the income divide in our country. There ought to be more focus on the educational divide.

Perhaps more than any other factors, the level and quality of a child's education determine his or her income potential. But it does much more. A good education teaches young people to think, to explore, to innovate, to set goals, to be personally responsible and disciplined, and to open their minds to the wider world of ideas and cultures.

To be sure, there are plenty of highly educated people in America who are rude and close-minded. Maybe you know some of them! But by failing so many of our young people through inferior education, who can deny that we are undermining their chance to participate fully, effectively and lawfully in the community?

Let me briefly mention two other factors that I believe are contributing to the decline of civility in American life. First is the proliferation of media outlets, entertainment opportunities and channels of instantaneous communication – all delivered to us courtesy of a ubiquitous and often anonymous Internet.

This is mostly a positive and empowering development. But we need to recognize and work on the downsides. It's easier now to self-select our news, clicking only on those opinions we already agree with. It's more tempting now to speak before we think, and to do so in short sensational bursts that provoke and even insult.

And given all the competition for eyes and ears, news and entertainment providers are often driven to the extremes of "shock and awe" in order to build audiences – which in turn has seriously lowered the standards of accuracy and good taste.

The last factor I'd mention – before discussing some possible solutions – is the reality that the American people are politically and philosophically divided almost 50-50 and have been for some time. In fact, recent polls have asked Americans whether they believe the federal government should do more or should it do less. Guess what? Half the country says more and half of it says less.

This divide has narrowed the political center to a sliver – any moderate New England Republican can tell you how lonely it feels out there! The decline of the political center has in turn amplified the more ideological voices on both sides, which doesn't exactly lend itself to tame and polite political discourse.

The result is a less civil, more bombastic political conversation that frankly disgusts many Americans and prevents our government from solving problems.

This is a challenge, but let's not wax too nostalgic about the past. Our politics have often been vicious from the very beginning. Jefferson once called Hamilton the "son of a whore" and Hamilton publicly exposed Jefferson's affair with his slave. During the debate over the abolition of slavery, one senator nearly caned his colleague to death on the Senate floor. And our nation did, after all, endure a bloody Civil War.

Incivility has long been a problem, but the imperative to address it has never been more urgent. When politicians posture, insult and demagogue, what happens? Americans tune out. Problems fester. Challenges go unmet. And our legacy as a can-do nation that embraces exciting ideas and bold solutions diminishes.

The Right to Speak ...
and the Responsibility to Listen

So let's talk about possible solutions.

I'd like to tell you that I have some new, groundbreaking insight to bring to this very complex debate. But I've learned over the years that complex and seemingly intractable problems cry out for the simplest solutions.

So my thought is this: We need to get back to the basics ... including reaffirming and strengthening two fundamental values – our right of free speech and our system of free enterprise. They are by no means cure-alls. But I'm convinced affirming these values will not only help restore civility in our country but also restore opportunity and freedom. In other words, the American Dream.

Let me begin with free speech. You can't rebuild civility without first recognizing and respecting everyone's right to speak. And free speech is more than just the right to say something – it's the right to speak with democratic influence, by which I mean the right to fully participate in the public and political affairs of our communities and our nation.

Intentionally or unintentionally, for good motives and bad, a lot of people are trying to over-regulate speech ... to constrain our ability to petition the government ... to impose overly restrictive speech codes on our campuses and other institutions ... and to even use powerful arms of the government, such as the IRS, to discriminate against speech they don't like.

We must vigilantly oppose and guard against attacks on free speech. And please understand – if we lose our constitutionally-protected right to speak, it won't be because we let some dictator yank it away, it will be because, collectively, we Americans let it slip away.

There's a reason why the right to free speech is the *First* Amendment to the Constitution. Our Founding Fathers understood its fundamental importance.

Let me give a few examples from my world on how speech is being stifled through fear, intimidation, and overregulation. Labor unions, shareholder activists and anti- business policymakers have long sought to drive the voice of the business community out of the political process and the public debate.

The Securities and Exchange Commission has been asked by these groups to make a rule that would compel public companies to disclose their spending on independent political speech. The idea here is to bring these companies' political spending – which *is* free speech – out into the open so they can be targeted for harassment and boycotts.

In 2010, some in Congress tried to sway the midterm elections in their favor through the DISCLOSE Act, legislation that would have chilled political participation by the business community – but not by labor unions. The bill was defeated. But business opponents still want to see its principles enacted, and some lawmakers are working to revive the legislation.

Proponents of such efforts claim that they are simply fighting for transparency. Don't be fooled. What they really want is to silence viewpoints they don't like in order to have a one-sided conversation with the American people in the public square. They aim to do this by regulating speech they don't like, and intimidating speakers they don't agree with.

Now, there are plenty of people who may be less than enthused with the business message on all issues. Well then, fight us on the ideas! Tell the American people we're dead wrong! But don't shut down and choke off our right – or the right of any other American citizen or institution – to speak up and speak out.

Most of our rights in a free society also carry responsibilities. This is especially true when it comes to speech. I strongly believe that the right to speak carries with it the responsibility to listen … to give others a fair hearing … to be open to different points of views.

In my view, it's the stubborn refusal to listen that is the cause of much of the incivility and dysfunction we see in Washington and across our country today.

Earlier, I mentioned the need for entitlement reform. That's a classic example of how a problem can get out of hand – not just because people disagree about solutions, but because most people refuse to even recognize there is a problem. They simply don't want to hear it.

Restoring civility in American life must begin by reaffirming our commitment to everyone's right to speak – *and* everyone's responsibility to listen.

Free Enterprise

We can also help restore civility by reaffirming our commitment to free enterprise and the growth, jobs and opportunities that free enterprise can deliver.

It's not perfect, but free enterprise is the best and, I would argue, the fairest and most civilized economic system ever devised. It offers more opportunity, more personal dignity, more freedom and more broadly shared prosperity than any other system.

Properly implemented, it strives to deliver equality of opportunity, not results. It recognizes and rewards the honor and dignity of all work, from blue collar to white collar and everything in between. It allows people to take a risk, fail and try again without being stigmatized. And when you succeed, you get rewarded.

This is the system that made America the strongest economy on earth. It's the system that makes the American Dream possible – and during this pivotal time for our nation, it's a system that deserves reaffirmation from all of us.

Free enterprise can help us address the most urgent need facing our country – more good-paying jobs. Recent employment reports have shown middling progress. But scratch beneath the surface, and a more disturbing picture emerges. The unemployment rate is dropping because people are giving up looking for work. The labor participation rate is at a 35-year low.

There is a whole class of people in their late 40s and early 50s who have been out of work for months and may never work again. Even college graduates are having difficulty finding jobs. As a result, they are postponing getting married and having children and falling behind financially.

Teen unemployment rates – especially for minorities – are through the roof. An entire generation of young people is at risk.

This is a serious matter for our society. It's about more than just getting a regular paycheck – it's about human dignity, being fully engaged in society, and being involved in something larger than yourself. It undercuts the American Dream – and it undermines civility.

That's why reaffirming our commitment to free enterprise and engaging its principles to create jobs and growth are so imperative. A robust, growing economy, powered by free enterprise, will not solve all of our problems, but it will lift our spirits and our sights. It can fund the improvements we must make in our schools, which is the best approach to reducing the inequality of income and of hope.

It will help us bridge the potential divide we face as we struggle to care for growing numbers of elderly, while also preserving and expanding opportunities for the young.

And it can put America back to work and help us recapture our legacy and leadership as an exceptional can-do country – a world leader with an economic and moral influence that is second to none.

Conclusion

Let me conclude where I started by saying that when it comes to restoring civility, we must all make a personal commitment.

I am frequently asked to address students or speak at their graduations. Often they're looking for some clues and secrets on how to achieve success.

I'm afraid that more often than not, I disappoint them because I want to leave them with a different message. What I most want to tell those young people is that when you reach a certain age where most of your life is behind you, what's going to really count? How will you be judged and remembered?

Not by the titles you held, the points you scored, or the money you made, but by the simple test of how you treated others – your family, your friends, the people who worked for you, and even the strangers on the street.

Treat them all with kindness and civility, speak thoughtfully and listen well, and go out of your way to teach and to help – with *no* expectation of anything in return.

If you do that, you just might get something in return – including better jobs, careers and livelihoods. But most of all, you will be building a reputation of honor and respect. You will get the most out of life, cement a lasting legacy, and make those you care about – and who care about you – very proud.

Georgette Mosbacher

On

Civility and the Art of Giving Thanks

W hen I was asked to talk about civility, I gave it a lot of thought, and the first thing I asked myself was, what does civility mean, and how would I define civility? And the more I thought about it, what I came to was manners. And I thought, is that an old-fashioned term? Why would manners be an old-fashioned term? But you don't really hear about it anymore, do you?

Growing up I learned manners by my mom slapping us on the hand or putting soap in our mouths, literally. That's how I learned it as a child. And so maybe it is old-fashioned, because I'm certainly old enough to be old-fashioned. But it shouldn't be old-fashioned.

Civility really should be thought of in the terms of manners. How do we treat other people? How do we behave with one another? How do we even behave when we're not in front of a big crowd? How do we behave with just one other person, our co-worker, our family?

You know that old cliché – and here we go again, old-fashioned – cliché about I should treat you how I want you to treat me. How did we forget that? Do you know anybody who doesn't want to be treated well? I don't, and yet I see it all the time.

I see people who behave in ways that are both embarrassing – and, as I really drilled down on it, there was another word that came to mind, and that was "shameful." Growing up where I grew up, you didn't behave in certain ways because you didn't bring shame on yourself, your family, your neighborhood, on your community. There were certain kinds of behaviour that you didn't do because you didn't bring shame on yourself. And it wasn't just about you. It was about the people you loved, the people you respected, and your neighbors.

I don't know what's happened to that idea of shame. I turn on the television and see these reality shows and I say, how can people behave like that? I walk through the airport and see the way people treat people, I listen to music lyrics, or go to the movie theater where some of the things that you see on the screen are just … I'm ashamed. I feel shame when I see it. I know it when I see it. And yet, we're bombarded by it.

And we're wondering where has civility gone? Have we been desensitized by all of this? I hope the answer is no, we haven't been. I hope that we still do feel that shame and we do understand what bad behavior is, and treating one another disrespectfully.

I was at dinner at someone's home – forget about being in a restaurant, it would be bad there too. We're all at one table and someone pulls out their BlackBerry and starts to text.

And I though to myself, here we go again. When I grew up we didn't have a telephone in our dining room because you didn't take a phone call when you ate. You just didn't do that! And yet, someone today can think it's OK, without insulting not only the person on their right and left but their hostess and everyone else at the table, to peck away at their cell phone? How did we drift that far?

I'm not embarrassed to tell anyone who sits at my table and pulls out a BlackBerry that it's just plain rude and an insult to me as the hostess, and not to do it. Maybe we need to be that blunt. Maybe we need to get back to that place where we're that frank.

Senator Olympia Snowe has said something that I want to repeat, because it is worth repeating: "Civility is really the mechanism by which you distill the varying viewpoints and philosophies in order to arrive at solutions. You have to accept the fact that you don't have a monopoly on good ideas and acknowledge the fact that you're not going to get what you want 100 percent of the time."

We don't see much of that today. All we have to do is look at our last presidential election. Here were two men running for the highest office in the land – one could argue in the world – and they were yelling at each other, pointing their fingers at each other, calling each other names. If our candidates for president can't act civilly, what do we expect from our youth and the next generations?

And yet, our democracy has civility built into it because every four years we have a peaceful transfer of power. Every four years, we argue, we go out there, we make up. We have differing points of view. Hopefully we can do that civilly.

And yet, we go to the polls and we have, by and large, free and fair elections, with very little incident. The military isn't called up; we don't have tanks in the street. We have civility built in to our very Constitution.

And so, you have to ask yourself, why do we witness this kind of behavior between leaders who should be setting the example for us? Leadership counts and how we behave counts.

My mother was widowed at 27. She had four children. My father was killed in an automobile accident. It threw us to the edge of poverty.

I was the oldest at age seven; my sister Lyn was two. I was raised by my mom, my grandmother and my great-grandmother, and they may not have known the definition of civility, but they did it by example.

These were three women who showed each other respect, and showed us respect. Now don't misunderstand me. My mother *would* wash our mouths out with soap. My mother would slap our hands. We were to respect our elders. There were codes of behaviour. But I learned by example.

Those very same women also taught me what it is to give back. The first example of that that I can remember is my great-grandma. She couldn't read or write, but she could count and she could bake. And at Easter, she would bake three loaves of bread. We kept one. I remember this so well because we would help her knead the bread – she was older and her hands weren't strong enough. So we would all do the kneading for her. It was a family thing. We'd bake these three loaves of bread.

The other two loaves were taken to church and they were blessed, and then they were left there. And they were left because we were told that the church would know who needed them. We needed them, actually, but as little as we had, there were people who had less.

That was my first recollection of that art of giving. And what it was rooted in was caring. The true art of giving is you have to care,

care about something enough. You have to care about something enough that you want to either share it or you want to help and make a difference.

How this is taught? I think you learn it as a child. I think that it comes with the examples that you set. But I think that we all have to set those examples.

I, as a CEO of a company, have a responsibility to my employees, how I treat them and how they're going to treat one another, because without that sense of treating someone else the way you want to be treated, it could be an awful place to go to work every day. As a CEO, I have a responsibility to set that tone, how I behave, how I treat others. And I do believe you can be civil and still make hard decisions, correct things, even sit someone down and say, "You didn't do this right." But you can do that in a way without being nasty.

And yet, today in our politics we don't see a lot of that. We don't see that sense of treating others with a respect and saying, "you know what, I don't have to be right all the time."

Peggy Noonan recently wrote in *The Wall Street Journal* that, "We are becoming a conceited, nitwit society, pushy and self-aggrandizing. No one is ashamed to brag now and show off. They think it heightens them. They think it's good for business. It used to be that if you were big, you never needed to tell people how big you were because that would be kind of classless and small. In fact, it would be proof of smallness."

"So," she wrote, "Don't be showy. The big are modest."

"Modest" – is that an old-fashioned word too? What happened to that? I turn on the TV and see 12-year-olds dressed in ways that my mother probably wouldn't have just slapped me on the hand. She would've taken me by the arm and dressed me. I don't know what's happened to modesty.

So we're back to civility and these old-fashioned terms. I actually miss them.

I think one of the most important facets of civility is to give back and show gratitude. And I think those who reach out, those who lend a hand, even those who stand up and advocate what they believe in a civil way, are giving back and showing that they care.

I am particularly involved with our veterans. It's not only because personally I care so much, it's also because I believe that it's a responsibility of every citizen.

We have an all-volunteer Army now, so most of us aren't touched by those who serve. But the fact is that we all do owe them a debt of gratitude. We all do owe them. We have a responsibility to take care of our veterans and their families.

I am not going to give you statistics that would truly be disturbing about the number of veterans who come home and commit suicide, except to just tell you that we can make a difference in their lives, and it's important that we do.

Many of our veterans have come back with catastrophic injuries and a lot of them with missing limbs. Fortunately, today, we have the technology to fit them with new arms and new legs. I will tell you about one young soldier who came home. He lost both of his arms. In my work with the Fallen Heroes Fund, we fitted him with two new arms, prostheses, and today we can even connect the nerve endings so they can actually feel.

But if I could share with you that moment when that young soldier held his baby in those two arms – well, this whole subject about giving, I got much more back. It was so rewarding. It's very easy to give when you get that kind of feedback.

And I'll tell you a story that is not quite as tangible. We were opening up a treatment and diagnostic center for catastrophic brain trauma. This is a real problem because it's not a wound that you can see. It's not a wound that most military people want to admit – that there's something wrong with them – because it isn't macho. And yet, it is the signature wound of the 21st century, so it's a real problem.

I was at Camp Lejeune, and we were breaking ground on one of these centers – and here's the great news that we can all feel good about. We raised $70 million, every penny from the private sector, to build it – every penny.

There were the drumrolls and "Pomp and Circumstance" and a tent where we went to for refreshments after we broke ground.

And there was a young man and he had a dog in his lap, and I am a dog lover myself, and so, I went up to him and asked him if I could pet the dog and he said, "You can," he said, "but he's a little under the weather today." Then he explained.

"You know, I could not have attended an event like this. I couldn't really go out really anywhere where there could be any noise or any sound that I didn't expect because I'd have a panic attack," he said. "But my dog has kind of the same problem. And today, I couldn't have been here, but the dog jumped in my lap and when he had a panic attack, I calmed the dog down.

"So everything's fine, but that's why he's a little under the weather."

And I realized at that instant, we'd given him that dog. He had gone through our facility and that dog was trained for a panic attack.

And so, when something triggered the young man's panic attack at the event, that dog jumped into his lap and did what it was supposed to, trained to do.

And how amazing that this young man could go back into normal life because we were able to recognize it, treat him, find out what was wrong, even though it was not a wound you could see, and then provide him with this dog. It was another one of those examples of what a difference you can make, and you don't even know.

You could have passed him at that event and never known that he was only there because we were able to provide him with that dog. You wouldn't have even known that, and you could have been responsible for helping him. Those are the intangibles.

Not long ago I received an email from the executive director of the Green Beret Foundation. We did their first fundraising event, and I chaired it. When you're raising money and it's not an event that's been established, you don't know how well you're going to do, and you're anxious. I called on all my friends and we worked hard at it, and it was a very successful event. The email read:

"Hello Ms. Georgette. You may have heard in the news that this past Thursday a train hit a float with several service members and spouses out in West Texas. They were in a parade that was kicking off a weekend for Hunts for Heroes. Two of the three casualties were Green Berets. They were killed and two spouses were very injured. We had three Green Berets in that parade. The other one was on a float in front of the one that was hit. My husband and I have known those folks for years. They were all in the same group. If it wasn't for the fundraising effort this year by you, your sister and all your most charitable and loving friends we would not be able to support this catastrophic tragedy. Just wanted to send a note to say thank you." Another example.

You never know in life what comes along. All my friends who pitched in, they'll never know. They'll never know that what they did changed these families that lost a husband, father, brother. They made a difference in their lives, and they'll never know that. I wouldn't have known that there were two Green Berets in that float had she not sent this email.

People always ask me, isn't the government supposed to take care of our veterans? And I say yes, they are but they don't, so we have to. I don't even try to explain anything more than that. That's all I know. They don't, so we have to. Just keep that in mind.

There are a lot of them coming home now. They're all coming home from Afghanistan and Iraq, and we have a big responsibility in front of us, a big one.

The art of giving is just caring. I don't know a better way to say it, except that you can do it in a lot of ways. You can do it with your time. You can do it with your intelligence. You can do it with your expertise. You can do it with your checkbook. There are a lot of ways to do it. The important thing is that you do it.

Joel Klein

On

Civility in Education

C ivility is a topic that I care very deeply about because I see it eroding in our schools. Indeed, civility is a thing that should be taught as important to participation in civil society.

You know, it's trite to say but deeply true: Civility costs us nothing and yet means so very much to all of us. You'd think something like that for free, we could get right.

In education, in politics, in law enforcement, in the arts or, business, or what have you, we all observe increased incivility in our country. It seems to be a symptom and not a disease in itself. Why is it that people seem to become increasingly shrill, that our public discourse is, more and more, filled with personal attacks and blame games, rather than problem-solving?

This is what concerns me greatly. I think we're at a precipice in America where we're going to have to answer a fundamental question about our country, and that is: Do the things that unite us as a people with a vision for tomorrow, are those things greater than the things that separate and divide us? I think that's the question that will decide whether we will engage in civil society, civil discussion and the kind of problem-solving that our country so desperately needs.

It's not just the past few years, but exacerbated by the recession in 2008 was a deep belief and a profound shift in most Americans' view, where they used to think their own lives would get better and their kids' lives would be better than their lives. That was really at our heart, what makes this country feel like we're tied together, this great hope that no matter how you struggled, how many jobs you had, how hard it was, your kids would lead a better life.

We call that the American Dream. And I must say that American Dream is now being eroded, and eroded at multiple levels. If you ask people today, a majority of Americans don't think their kids' lives will be better than theirs, and they don't think their own lives are getting any better. And when you live with that kind of frustration, you start to see the world through a different prism.

I was privileged to recently do a report with Secretary Condoleezza Rice for the Council on Foreign Relations, and I was very impressed by the words she wrote: "The United States is an exceptional nation, in many ways. As a people, we are not held together by blood, nationality and ethnicity or religion. The true American identity is born of the idea that it does not matter where you came from. It only matters where you're going. That animating spirit brought people from all over the world."

We were the magnet for immigration. People came here - and I met literally thousands and thousands of them in the public schools in New York - because they wanted a better life for their kids. And as long as they believed that, then the glue held together. In this report that Secretary Rice and I chaired for the Council on Foreign

Relations, we put in play that the failure to succeed in education will mean that, in fact, the American dream will no longer be the glue that binds us.

Two facts are really troubling. One, we used to have high upward mobility in America. You could come from nowhere, as Condoleezza Rice said, and go anywhere. Right now, we are one of the least upwardly mobile countries in the entire world. Europe has eclipsed us. And I'll give you one statistic. If you look at the top 200 colleges in America, almost three-quarters of the kids who go there come from the top quarter of the income spectrum. And about four or five percent come from the bottom quarter. So we're not seeing that mobility that unites us. And, as a result, frustration is increasing.

People are talking about makers and takers. That's the divide. But we're in this together, folks. We're not makers and takers. We really have to understand that those kids may not be your kids literally, but they are your kids, because they grow up in a world in which hope is replaced by despair and opportunity is replaced by increasing frustration, and if you think we're seeing instability now, you can't imagine what's going to come. We need to be in this together.

When I see people talk about the 99 percent versus 1 percent, it really sticks in my craw, people are the 100 percent. It's not a "we-they" world. It's an "us" world. And what's the implication of that 99 to 1, that somehow that 1 percent, the very successful people, the people that used to be the pinnacle of the American dream, somehow don't deserve it. You see, it's harder to aspire and look up if you think you're locked in and your kid doesn't have that kind of future.

That's borne of a frustration that we feel about whether we're going to get ours in a land in which we're increasingly seeing the pie as fixed in how it get divided – you pay more taxes, she gets fewer benefits, etc. – rather than a vision that says the American dream is vibrant and alive.

I think the Internet actually exacerbates this problem. When I went to college I tried to read several newspapers every day, and I read editorial pages I agreed with and some I didn't agree with. Today, people go to the sites they like that share the same views, and they get each other all talked up and wound up. That reinforces one's views.

There is a study in education involving two of the most popular websites, one virtually on one side of the debate, and one on the other side. They studied it, and almost no one, even though these are two enormously popular Websites, visits both.

So in a world in which there's increased frustration and anxiety about the future, coupled with a world in which we can reinforce our ideas through social networks and new media and the Internet, we're really starting to grow, gradually but steadily, apart.

When you go to a public hearing now, it's not about solving the problem. Every community has problems, every school system has its problems. It's not about people sitting there and coming together and saying, okay, we've got to do a better job educating our kids. We all know that.

What's it about? People pointing fingers at each other, ascribing blame, people trying to shout each other down. I used to be amazed when I was chancellor of the New York public school system. I'll be the first to tell you that not everything I did was a great idea. I tried some stuff that didn't work, and sometimes, like anybody else, I just whiffed when I swung at the ball.

But the amount of disrespect that grew in the system…, well I was amazed that people would do this in a roomful of children. I mean, just the message you're sending to these kids, and it became so deep.

So rather than being the edifice on which we build civil society, the education system is becoming the crucible on which we destroy it, because fundamental respect for institutions, for leadership, is not taught. When I see somebody, no matter who he is, say, while the president of the United States is delivering the State of the Union Address, "You lied," that's unimaginable to me.

This is not to say we shouldn't disagree – and let me be clear - disagreement is the grist for development, change and evolution. And people should feel passionately. And I don't think there's anybody who feels more passionately about education reform than myself. But passion and incivility don't necessarily have to go hand-in-hand. And we have got to figure out a way to have the passion without the incivility.

There are two core principles I try to honor. The first is, as a matter of humility, if not as a matter of candor, no matter how strongly you believe about something, you may not be right. None of us has a monopoly on wisdom and virtue. And a lot of us have changed our minds.

One of the leading proponents in the education debate literally did 180-degree flip on things like charter schools, accountability, and so forth. And now she's a strong proponent on the other side. And while it's great that she says she changed her mind and she evolved – I respect that –she should remember she might change her mind again. She might learn more things. A little bit of humility always helps.

The second principle is to keep the focus on the merits, on the issues. Even if we have a serious disagreement about the role of charter schools, that's a respectable disagreement, but to try to personalize it or go into motives, or try to undermine people because of honest policy disputes becomes increasingly destructive. And when you get on that path, you can stay for a long, long time.

One example really bothers me because I think it so reflects how we're going in wrong direction. There are a number of large philanthropies that are very active in educational reform, one run by Bill Gates, one run by Michael Bloomberg, the Walton Foundation, Eli Broad in California. So the people who don't like some of their ideas have now come to call those people the "billionaires boys club." Now, this is clearly meant to be derogatory and to suggest two things: one, that these people somehow have an economic interest in school reform, and, second, that because they're billionaires, somehow, they shouldn't be allowed to use their philanthropy to support change.

Now, when these same exact people are spending major philanthropic dollars to cure malaria or AIDS, nobody would call them the billionaire boys' club. They don't get anything in return for trying to cure AIDS. Indeed, one of the great things about America, unique in the world, is the amount of philanthropy we have seen from our most fortunate citizens. Yet, in the education debate, they have come to be denigrated.

And that's emblematic of the fact that instead of joining an issue on the merits, people would rather, particularly in a Twitterati era, rather shoot out 140 characters and be electric and trashy and so forth. It has now become part of the discussion and the debate in education, at a time when we should all, whatever our disagreements, be pulling together, because our current education system is not going to get us where we need to go in the 21st century.

Today in America, if we had an honest high school graduation rate, that rate would be about 35 percent. The College Board says about 22 percent of our kids are fully college ready. So we have a long road ahead of us. And I want to tell you, I travel the world, and the people in Korea and in Japan, Singapore, Brazil, and elsewhere, are not going to wait around while we get our education act together.

So talking about civility matters, but if we don't address the underlying issues about a society in which upward mobility and social mobility are increasingly becoming less, and a society in which more and more people, every year, are thinking that their kids' lives won't be better than theirs. We need the kind of leadership in Washington that doesn't say we shouldn't have a sequester tomorrow, but we nevertheless have a sequester tomorrow. Whether you're for cuts or against cuts, everybody thinks this is the wrong way to do it.

In the long run, there's only one solution to the problems that we're discussing, to the underlying anxieties, and that solution is to make a different kind of bet on K-12 education. If we have a system in which the haves are the ones that are going to go to great college and the have-nots are the ones that fall further and further behind, we will see a hollowing out of the middle class.

In the first half of the 20th century, we were the first country in the world to insist on secondary education; every kid had to go to high school. After World War II, we were the country with the G.I. scholarships that increased our college-going dramatically. Now that's all stopped. Our college-going and college graduation rate is falling behind the rest of the world. We are not getting the successes we need. And that will lead to a hollowing out of the middle class.

If that happens, and if you think public discourse today is coarse, wait until you see what will come. Frustrated people become angry people. And angry people are not civil people.

And so, for me, the reason I have spent the last 10 years of my life working on education is I think this is America's challenge. I don't think we can have a ZIP Code system of education. I don't think we can have a system where kids in middle class and affluent communities are getting different opportunities.

I always used to say when I was Chancellor, look, if you're rich and you want to have a big house and a big car and a boat and all of that, whatever floats your boat is fine with me. But your kids shouldn't get a better education than my kid. That's a different thing. That's the thing that levels us and integrates us and holds us together. That is the glue.

And I think it's past time to stop pointing fingers, stop yelling and screaming, trying to ascribe blame and label people "billionaire boys' club," and understand it's going to take the entire country working together with our greatest talents, hoping that our best people go in to teach.

When I think about the teaching profession in America, I want it to be everyone's hero. In Japan, a teacher is called "sensei," which represents a dignified learning professional, and they are at the pinnacle of where people are respected as learned professionals. In America, we don't have that.

I want to see schools that are new and different, that challenge our kids in different ways, and I want to see technology that really supports and excites our teachers. We ask a lot from our teachers. There's no reason we can't give them the kinds of help and support and tools and programming that will enable them to take their game to a different level.

This is all doable, unless we want to sit around and point fingers and yell and scream at each other, and see if we can come up with labels and names and criticisms based on the fact that you're fortunate enough to have made it in America and willing to give a whole hell of a lot back through philanthropy. Those are the real options. And I must say, given the bickering we're getting now at the national level, I worry about whether we can pull together to meet these challenges.

A friend of mine who I admire enormously, Tom Brokaw, wrote a book about the greatest generation, and I think about it all the time when I think about where we are in 21st century America. As Tom explained, the greatest generation was prepared to go to war to save the world from an existential threat. But today we face a new existential threat, and it's not one that an army can save us from. It's being driven by complacency about a school system that is failing our children. And it is high time we come together to do something about it.

So, for our generation, the question is not would you put your life on the line, the question is will the American dream become the American memory on our watch?

So much less is asked of us, and yet, we seem now unwilling to do it. We want to make sure that in this pie, which is fixed or shrinking, we get our piece. And if we continue in that way, I promise you the things that made this country the greatest country in the world will slowly, but inevitably, slip away.

And there's no place more important than in education – I'll leave you with this simple thought: When I was Chancellor, I had about 1,700 schools that I was responsible for in New York City. I used to go to meetings like this and I used to say to people, candidly, how many of my 1,700 schools would you send your own kids to? The most I ever got was about 20 percent, about 350. More typically, I got about 100 or 200. And I used to say to them, whose kids should go to the other 1500 schools? And they used to say, other people's children. I developed an acronym. I called them OPCs.

But, you see, folks, those aren't other people's children. Those are our children. And so long as there's a kid in America who's going to a school that you wouldn't send your kids to, then the American dream is being chipped away and eroded.

The Hon. Rick Perry

On

Civility in Modern Society

When I take economic development trips, spreading the word about Texas' economic climate, some state officials can get a little, well, testy.

I recall one trip to a very large, very prominent state out west not too long ago and the governor of that state compared my efforts to a certain, embarrassing bodily function. It rhymes with "cart." That was actually funnier than it was mean, but even to a guy raised on a farm, it was a bit on the crude side.

Civility has been an American ideal dating back to this country's origins. Ben Franklin once said, "Be civil to all, sociable to many, familiar with few, friend to one, enemy to none." I'm not sure I entirely agree with everything he said there, but you get the gist of his point.

The problem is, while it's been an American ideal, we haven't consistently been able to live up to it all that well. And, maybe it's just me, but it seems it's getting worse lately, too.

Maybe it's got something to do with a permanent campaign culture, where everything is broken down into the simplest component – who won and who lost. It's horse race politics, where even compromises are assigned winners and losers.

Maybe it's an increasingly fractured media landscape, where saying the most outrageous things is the only sure-fire way to guarantee attention, or maybe by marrying a Kardashian.

And the Internet certainly isn't helping matters.

The Internet grants people anonymity – giving them a sense of action without accountability. And its instantaneous nature lends itself to people saying the wrong thing at the wrong time, filter-free. Twitter and Facebook spreads rumors at lightning speed, and if enough people re-tweet or "like" something, rumors go from "unsubstantiated" to "fact" in the blink of an electronic eye.

Recall Churchill's old line: "A lie gets halfway around the world before the truth gets a chance to put its pants on?" These days, a lie can make it twice around the world before the truth even gets a Google news alert that there's a problem. So we've got anonymity, combined with an easy, widespread distribution system.

Read enough misinformation about someone, and you begin to develop a false sense that you know them, even if you've never met them, or spoken to them, in your life. Once we think we know somebody, and we've assigned them all these negative ideas, it's all too easy to vilify that person – and to assign villainous motives.

It's not enough to disagree with someone's politics. In our dialogue today you pretend to know what's in someone's heart. It's just a high-tech way to dehumanize someone with a different viewpoint. Again, it's nothing new, but the Web makes it easier and more widespread.

Einstein once said, "It has become appallingly obvious that our technology has exceeded our humanity." But that's not an excuse for our uncouth behavior. Technology didn't get us into this all by itself, and it certainly can't get us out of it.

We've all contributed to the coarsening of the public discourse, myself included.

You'd be hard-pressed to find someone who's beaten up on Washington, D.C., more than I have over the past few years. But part of the reason people bash Washington is *because* of a lack of civility, which profoundly contributes to its dysfunction. They get nothing done because they can't even communicate to one another except by press conference.

The important thing to remember, though, is that civility is a choice. No matter what we think may be driving us to name-calling, or fear mongering, or snarky comments, we are making a conscious choice – a conscious choice to depart from our values.

Nobody understood that better than Ronald Reagan. President Reagan was the quintessential Happy Warrior; someone who would fight passionately for what he believed in, but with a smile on his face and love in his heart. His close friendship with his political opposite, Speaker of the House Tip O'Neill, has become the stuff of legend. It was made easier by the fact that these were two charismatic individuals with good hearts and open personalities. But they were very different men, who made a priority of building and maintaining their friendship, and it was through that friendship that a lot of great things were accomplished for the United States.

These were lessons not lost on his successor – my fellow Texan, President George H.W. Bush. I can tell you from personal experience, you'd have to work hard to find a kinder, gentler individual. He showed respect and fairness to everyone, Republican or Democrat.

That's because he understood that while coarseness can score political points, civility is what brings people together to get things done. We can accomplish so much more by learning to listen to our opponents, to understanding the way they see the world.

We can do so much more by committing ourselves to an open climate, where people can voice opinions without fear of being shouted down – or called a name – or given a label that can permanently stain a reputation. We can do so much more by accepting the fact that we can't, in the end, win 'em all, and not nurse grudges that could further spoil and pollute our discourse.

Please notice, none of this means we have to change what we believe. None of this means we don't fight hard for what we think is best for our state, or for our country. None of this means we're weak or ineffective if we don't get dragged, kicking and screaming, from the public arena. It just means there's a better way of going about this.

There had better be, because it's the only way to truly heal our nation. America is a huge nation, filled with a diverse population with very different ideas and feelings about everything. That's certainly true in Texas.

The people in North Texas are very different from the people in South Texas, the people in East Texas are very different from the people in West Texas. Heck, the people in Austin are different from the people in – well, everywhere else in Texas.

Our solution in Texas has been to ensure that local governments have the most authority in the most matters. We hold to the idea that local people are in the best position to solve local problems, certainly better positioned than people hundreds, or even thousands, of miles away.

The idea that any one perspective, emanating from Washington D.C., the Texas Capitol, or anywhere else, for that matter, can satisfy all of those diverse viewpoints and meet all those needs all by itself – is folly.

None of us can do it alone. *All* of us need to work together, accept differences and bridge gaps. The only way that can be done is by treating each other with the respect and civility we each deserve. We need to return to the value of grand ideas, solid policy and sound reasoning.

You don't need to lower the discourse if you have ideas you believe in.

Love and joy should be our code. Conviction and passion should lead to compassion, not contempt, anger or fear-mongering. We should stand for the principles that made America great, and exude those principles with joy.

Smile when you disagree. Be strong and courageous, while being loving and compassionate.

We can make America more than the freest and most prosperous nation on the face of the earth. We can make it into what Mr. Reagan described as "a shining city on a hill…that is an example to all."

Ecclesiastes 4:12 says, "A person standing alone can be attacked and defeated…but two men can stand back-to-back and conquer." It is time we once again had one another's back again.

The Hon. Olympia Snowe

On

Civility in Politics

Throughout my nearly 40 years in public office, I have witnessed government's greatest potential. I've also experienced the capacity for calamitous dysfunction. It's profoundly regrettable that the ever-increasing partisanship in Washington has prevented us from achieving a consensus, precisely at this moment in the life of America.

I'll be plain on one point, and that is I'm not leaving the United States Senate because I no longer believe in its potential or its possibility, or because I no longer love the institution. But I'm leaving precisely because of it.

I want to return the United States Senate to a bastion of thoughtful reasonable deliberation, so that we can achieve solutions to the problems that are facing our great nation. I want to take the fight in a different direction, outside of the United States Senate, but to return it to a refuge that is a sanctuary from the passions of politics, to restore our founding fathers' vision that it becomes a forum for not stoking the political fires but actually tempering them.

And so, that is my goal and that is my journey. And if there's one message that I want to convey to you, it is this – that we do not have to accept this all or nothing, win at all costs ever-increasing partisan atmosphere to be the new norm. We can reverse the tide of gridlock and ideological absolutism.

Now, the atmosphere is lamentable, but I happen to believe that is not irreparable. So why is civility so important to the political process? What makes it significant in restoring our political institutions? I can't tell you how many people have approached me, after I announced my decision, not only from within Maine but all across the country, and told me first that they expressed disappointment that I was not going to be in the Senate because of my moderate voice, but also because they were angry and fed up with the partisan bickering –

But they didn't understand that this partisan bickering is fueling the legislative deadlock. So the question is, how did the political processes in Washington become so jammed with the monkey wrenches of incivility and entrenchment?

There are so many factors that enter into the equation. It is, of course, the sensationalism that goes with the media today, in many respects, and it becomes the enemy of civility.

You have the insatiable appetite of having to feed the ratings and the content as generated by the 24-hours news cycle and social media. That serves to incite the demonization of differing viewpoints, not to mention it hardens the positions of policymakers from the outset, so it never gives them the opportunity to take a position or to engage in thoughtful debate on the United States Senate floor. Before we even have the opportunity to have a chance to debate the issue or to consider an issue, positions have already hardened, and they're never in a position to even consider the legislation in order to address it from multiple perspectives, because so much has changed in the process itself.

And so, as I have often said, everything is viewed through the prisms of MSNBC, on one hand, and Fox News, on the other.

And then, of course, you have the explosion of the third-party groups that are now funded by one or many advocates who are unyielding in their adherence to a single point of view or ideology, and they can bankroll enormous sums of money to flood the airwaves with invective that can determine the outcome of the campaigns all across this country. It gets worse with every election.

Illustrative of that point, 71 percent of the activities that they underwrite serve to oppose a candidate, rather than to support a candidate. In 1990, these organizations spent about $7 million. Today, it is closer to 452 million, so far in this election cycle, so it's 63 times the amount that was spent in 1990.

So what is the cumulative effect of all that? Well, there's a spillover into the halls of Congress, where we had virtually abandoned policymaking. There's no question, we're still fighting the last election, and from the last election we're fighting for the next election. And we have all these "gotcha" votes to advance one side and to disadvantage the other, and it's all designed for political leveraging.

It used to be that in the first year after the election, it was customary to focus on the issues that were important to the country, understanding in the second year of the session that, in all likelihood, politics would intercede as you got closer to the election.

But now, it's all about designing messaging amendments, and these messaging amendments aren't aimed at solving a problem, rather, it's about making sure that you get somebody on record with a recorded vote and then they can use that for fodder in the next 30-second sound bite for the 32nd ad that's going to be used in the next election.

So there was a time that we would govern, but now it has become a perpetual campaign. And it's not lost on most Americans because, after all, they've pegged Congress with the lowest approval rating. We have about a 10 percent approval rating.

We have counted 90 percent of the American people as disapproving of Congress' performance. And you would think that, in and of itself, would have galvanized and motivated Congress to get to work, but hardly.

So, indisputably, words matter because they set the tone and the tenor of our political conversations within the institutions, as well as outside. You know, every day in the United States Senate, when we're addressing the Senate and our fellow colleagues, we always say "My esteemed colleague, my good friend." That's a very worthy practice, but it never carries over to results, so we have the least productive Congress since 1947.

Civility also includes the idea of respecting one another's views and talking to people with whom you disagree, because I don't know of any other way. When I was still in the midst of my re-election, I would say to people, you know, I just don't understand how you solve a problem – whether it's in political life, personal life or professional life – when you're not going to talk to somebody with whom you disagree. How do you solve it?

And you have to accept the fact that you don't have a monopoly on good ideas and maybe knowledge the fact that you're not going to get 100 percent of what you want.

We don't agree 100 percent of the time. That's an idealism. So we have to learn how to transcend our differences, in order to make the system work. And that's what civility is all about. Civility is really the mechanism by which you distill the varying viewpoints and the philosophies in order to arrive at solutions.

I know that that sounds very quaint of a notion in today's political environment, especially one that is defined by coarse partisanship and what I describe as "podium thumping belligerence." But there was a time when it did work differently.

When I started in the legislature, both the Maine House and then the State Senate, after the election, we would put the campaign labels and our parties behind us and set to work on the issues that were important to our constituencies, because that's what it was all about. We were supposed to solve problems. That's the essence of public service, which we have lost sight of.

People ask me all the time, was it different, can it be different? I say, yes, it can be different and yes, it was different. When I arrived in the U.S. House of Representatives back in 1979, I joined what was then the Congresswoman's Caucus on Women's Issues. And it was formed initially by then-Congresswoman Elizabeth Holtzman, who was a pro-choice Democrat, and Congresswoman Margaret Heckler, who was a pro-life Republican. And despite their differences, they would not draw lines in the sand when it came to issues that were important to women and working families, because there were too few women in Congress. We were too under-represented. There were only sixteen of us in the House and one in the United States Senate.

And, at that time, the federal laws were working against women, in fact, discriminating against women, because they didn't reflect the dual roles and responsibilities of women, both at home and an ever-increasing number in the workplace. And so, we set about to change all that, and I became co-chair for a decade. And we passed child-support enforcement laws; family medical leave became the law of the land. We prohibited the cancellation of pensions without notification and without your spouse's approval. We ensured that federally funded clinical study trials didn't systematically exclude women and minorities, trials that made the difference between life and death. We supported childcare, making it accessible and making it affordable.

The point is our inherent bipartisanship and principle transcended our differences and became the foundation, and we made a difference.

When I arrived in the United States Senate after the election in 1994, there were still collegial, cooperative vestiges of collaboration, people still working across the political aisle. I joined what was then the Centrist Coalition, and I eventually co-chaired it with then John Breaux in 1999, and then with Joe Lieberman in the early 2000s.

After the government shutdown at the end of 1995, we began to meet during that volatile atmosphere to demonstrate that a large bipartisan group of us could get together and to craft a bipartisan balanced budget, and that we would offered it on the floor, so that we could display the ability to continue to work together, even in spite of that difficult and tumultuous time.

We offered it on the floor of the Senate and it didn't prevail, but we came close, and it shocked everybody that it became a prelude for the balanced budget that passed the subsequent year, and which we produced four consecutive years of surpluses, for the first time since 1930.

And then in 2005, another example of when people are determined to solve a problem. There was the "Gang of 14" that was organized, and I was part of it. It was seven Democrats and seven Republicans. And it was to avert an institutional crisis with the repeated systematic filibusters of then President Bush's judicial nominees.

On the Republican side, we were proposing the so-called "nuclear option," of which the net effect would have been to eliminate the 60 votes to end the filibuster. But that 60-vote threshold is a bulwark to protect minority rights in the United States Senate, and it would have long-term consequences on the institution, had we moved in that direction.

So we were able to agree to a compromise before we crossed that political Rubicon. We said we would oppose the filibustering of any judicial nominee unless it was warranted because of extraordinary circumstances, and, therefore, we would oppose also the exercising of the nuclear option.

So, in other words, each of us would make our own determination whether or not a judicial nominee posed extraordinary circumstances, which we would filibuster. But it worked because it forced all of us to think about truly did this nominee warrant a filibuster. We reached this agreement and paved the way for the judicial nominees to go forward. This decision and this agreement was made in keeping with the best traditions of the United States Senate.

Imagine today any of these scenarios unfolding in the United States Congress, in the political environment of 2012. But it's precisely that "can do" collaborative spirit that is required. Amy Gutmann, who is the president of the University of Pennsylvania, wrote in her book, The Spirit of Compromise, that we cannot escape compromise, but that politicians are likely to continue down this stark divisive path. Yet, that government and elected officials need to reach an agreement, if they are expected to govern well.

Unfortunately, what we're experiencing with some the red states getting redder and the blue states getting bluer is that that is also having a net effect in the institutions, in both the House and Senate. In 1987, there were 57 senators who were of one party affiliation but their states voted for the opposing presidential candidate. Today, there are only 25.

For example, my colleague and I are Republicans in Maine but our state has voted Democratic in the last five presidential elections. But the fact is, however, that you have 75 percent of the Senate with less political incentive to cross the political aisle for fear of risking or inviting a primary challenge.

That polarization has manifested itself in other ways. The National Journal conducted a survey, starting back in 1982, in which they showed that 58 senators came between the most liberal Democrat and the most conservative Republican. Today, there are zero.

That means there is no Democrat that is more conservative than a Republican and there's no Republican that is more liberal than a Democrat. So you're not having any crossovers, and there is no ability to form a coalition to cross over because you're not given the opportunity anymore in the United States Senate to modify the legislation and build the coalitions in which to accomplish that.

Even our founding fathers had a concern about undue allegiance to political parties. Alexander Hamilton and James Madison specifically cited it in the Federalist Papers. And to underscore where we are today, three political scientists released a study that indicated we have the highest level of polarization since the end of Reconstruction. That gives you an indication of the depths to which we have reached when it comes to the divisions that have obviously impeded our ability to do what's right.

I've witnessed firsthand how this political gulf has affected our ability to cross over and to do what's right for the best interest of this country. We can't even pass budgets. We're required by law to pass a federal budget by April 15th, the timeline and the deadline for all of us to file our tax returns. And yet, we have not passed a federal budget in the last three years, in the same three years in which we have had the highest deficits in our nation's history.

And you might ask why: It's because they don't want senators casting politically-sensitive votes. Well, I didn't get the memo where it says you get elected so you can do the easy stuff. But the fact is the Senate was designed uniquely to address issues, and now we've become more of a parliamentary system, where we move in political blocs, rather than having the opportunity to address each of these questions and being able to amend the bills that come before the United States Senate.

Every time we depart and diverge from the norms and traditions of the United States Senate, we contradict original purposes of the United States Senate, when it was initially created. For example, we have a traditional open amendment process, but even that has changed. And hence, that's the reason why we can't build those coalitions, because if you can't have amendments, there's no way to bring people in from both sides, from the right or from the left and more toward the middle.

Now, the Majority Leader has been exercising his right to fill the amendment tree 67 times since 2007, and what that means is, is that he will hand-select the amendments that will be offered, and even sometimes on the part of the minority. And so, as a result, we don't have the opportunity to offer those amendments.

The six previous majority leaders collectively didn't do this 40 times over a span of 22 years, from 1985. And you can see how dramatically that has changed. So the voices of millions of Americans that are represented by those United States senators.

When the parties don't get their way, they threaten to filibuster, and on it goes because we have more votes on filibusters to end filibusters.

When I arrived in the Senate in 1995, we had 161 cloture votes to end filibusters. In 2000, in my second term, we had 164. And in 2012, so far, we've 271. That's increase of 65 percent over that period of time, so it's become a burgeoning problem, especially in the United States Senate that was designed to be able to deliberately sort through the issues, so each other employs the others' tactics. If they were in the minority and then they become the majority, they use the majority's tactics, and the majority will use the minority's tactics, and they switch position from election to election. And on it goes.

That is the atmosphere in which we produced the worst political and financial brinkmanship, with the way in which we handled the debt ceiling crisis in 2011. That's a crisis that was manufactured. We could have ended that. We could have begun the process in January of 2011 because the initial timeline was in March. Then it was deferred to May and then ultimately to August. But, as you well know, we deferred to the 11th hour in August, and that sent shockwaves not only across the country but around the globe, and it precipitated the first credit downgrade ever in the history of our country.

It also produced the highest level of policy uncertainty over the last 20 years. A study was conducted by three political scientists that indicated that of all of the events that occurred over the last 20 years, including the Persian Gulf, September 11th, the Iraq War, the financial crisis, the debt ceiling crisis surpassed all of them.

Now, of course, you have the impending fiscal Cliff. That is another artificially generated crisis, because the tax cuts expired last December but they were temporarily deferred to the lame duck session. So now we have a combination of tax increases and spending cuts totaling $600 billion that will have to be considered at the end of this year, in the 36-day lame duck session, in conjunction with the debt ceiling limit increase, once again, and, of course, all of the other automatic cuts that already had been set in motion by the sequestration for the first year in 2013.

If we fail to act, that could likely trigger a recession, according to Chairman Bernanke and the Congressional Budget Office. But again, these are issues that could all have been handled in a systematic timely fashion because we certainly had the time on the Senate calendar to grapple with these questions.

So often I say, in the Senate we're surrounded by history but we're not inspired by it to reach to the height that we're capable of achieving, that we've somehow miniaturized the Senate instead of maximizing its potential to achieve the best that our country deserves.

I was reading in the Washington Post about this artist who bought some ad space in a Metro station in D.C. to illustrate his World War II style posters. The Washington Post described it as his crusade to return civility to our political discourse. He was quoted in the story as saying that he had a discussion with political wonks and they said, "This will never change, get used to it." And he said, "Get used to it? I never liked it and I won't get used to it."

And that's exactly right. We should not be countenancing or allowing those who literally are invested in the status quo to prevail in the final analysis. Bipartisanship isn't a political theory, it's a political necessity, to get things done for this country, and especially at this moment in time. So what it requires of all of as Americans is essentially to create a political reward for those who are willing to search for a common goal and a political penalty for those who don't.

I'm in the process of writing a book as a call to arms to reclaim our government and to harness the awesome power of the social media. Just like all the other movements have built in America and around the globe, the same could be true when it comes to building a movement for unity and doing what's right as an elected official.

So I have designed a PAC called Olympia's List, and I am going to support candidates who are consensus builders and believe in consensus building, as I do, because it is so critical to this country and to its future. We cannot allow this culture to be ingrained.

It's not a question whether or not it's a Republican idea or a Democratic idea or an independent idea. It's a question of whether or not it is a good idea. It's not what's in the best interest of a single party. It's what's in the best interest of the United States of America and for all of us.

When I think about the United States Constitution, the document that we revere and we cherish, it wasn't the fact that they were 55 people who came together and ratified the document because they all had the same viewpoint and they gathered in a room and rubber-stamped unanimous thinking – far from it. But what they recognized was the enormity and the gravity of the circumstances that necessitated the courage to achieve the consensus for their common goal for a stronger united America. And that's what it's all about.

So I see the foundation to rebuild government, to make it work, with the proliferation of so many groups and forums. There is a multiplicity of organizations that are developing all across the country because of their abiding concern over the lack of civility at all levels of government, in all spheres of life. Our future depends on it.

We have a group on the Democratic side that is called the Third Way, trying to bring Democrats to the middle. Republicans have a group called the Main Street Partnership to bring Republicans to the middle. You have the No Labels group that wants to take politics from the point-scoring to the problem-solving. You have the Americans Elect, on how we elect candidates.

I happened to meet the incredibly courageous Gaby Giffords recently, and her remarkable husband, Mark Kelly, and they have worked to establish the National Institute for Civil Discourse that's based in Arizona. And I agreed to join their board.

This is a concern all over America, and we have the underpinnings to put civility and compromise and consensus back into government, to make it work. It will require a concerted effort, without question, but it means channeling the social media such as my website, www.olympiaslist.org, and the overall media to engage millions of Americans, as we're all engaged in the idea of making our elected officials accountable and giving them the political strength to go to their leaders and to demand that they allow a process that will forge solutions that represent the very best of America.

Because it isn't about one person or one platform or one party. It truly is about the *United* States of America.

Ernie Anastos

On

Civility in Media

In all the years that I have been in broadcasting – 40 to be exact – I have been asked thousands of questions about covering news, anchoring programs, interviewing world leaders and celebrities and, yes, the glamour and excitement of it all. But I cannot remember anyone – on a street, in a classroom, at a dinner party – ever asking how news people behave and whether that behavior reflects our society.

So, when I was approached to talk about civility in the media – it came as a surprise. And it certainly made me think: Does civility exist in broadcasting and, if it doesn't – why not?

It's not an easy question and the answer is not a simple yes or no. My memory takes me back to my earliest days behind a microphone when I worked at a small radio station while going through high school.

That's where I began learning the very foundation of journalism – accuracy, truth and fairness.

Those principles have always stayed with me, from serving as a news assistant to the legendary Walter Cronkite at CBS to recently having the unique public responsibility as an owner of a group of radio stations. I was blessed to be able to see my career path.

From the moment that I walked into a newsroom at WRKO radio in Boston, I knew I was in a different world – clearly a strange place where all the stress of society found a home. I was out of college, a kid from Nashua, New Hampshire, about to get my first lesson in professional journalism.

From that point on, newsrooms became my second home and some of the characters in them were priceless mentors to me.

The newsrooms where I have worked – for the most part – do not fit the definition of civility. They are generally loud, peppered with colorful language, rarely well-organized, littered with used coffee cups, pizza boxes and some newspapers.

It has always been a wonder to me that somehow, this environment manages to lead to creativity and responsibility in communicating with a mass audience.

When we hit the air – and go into millions of homes, it has to be with respect for those who watch and listen. We should be careful not to offend in any way and always aware of the trust placed in us.

At times, however, politeness bumps up against the demands of reporting and the urgency to get the facts ahead of everyone else.

How, for example, can we balance civility and privacy with the aggressiveness of a reporter and the immediacy of television?

We all have seen instances where a reporter will stick a microphone in the face of a person in anguish who has just lost a friend or relative and ask questions that violate privacy and make us squirm.

And, there also are times when an attempt at civility doesn't work at all on the air. A number of years ago, we began introducing reporters – live at the scene of a story by saying: "good evening" and they would reply the same. It was a nice touch – a display of politeness between the anchor and reporter. But, you can imagine how awkward that can be if the story is a fire, a murder or anything but good.

To me, history and tradition are marvelous teachers. I wish young people heading into our business would spend as much time studying the events and personalities of the past as they do on technology and social media.

What a rich heritage we have in broadcasting – Edward R. Murrow, Peter Jennings and Walter Cronkite, once voted the most trusted man in America. Remember Chet Huntley and David Brinkley – nice to hear them say – "Good Night, Chet…" "Good Night, David." They were our heroes and we stand on their shoulders.

There were also rules in the early days of broadcasting – unwritten for the most part – but they were respected standards nevertheless that showed the kind of society we were. On the air, Edward R. Murrow would often refer to members of his reporting staff as "Mister Collingwood" or "Mister Severeid." This was civility with a touch of dignity.

And there was more.

For example, it was unthinkable for a journalist to interrupt a president while speaking. At that time it was considered rude, it was un-civil.

The media aside, other things were different too.

Men tipped their hats to women, kids obeyed their parents and cops on the street. It was another time – a different age.

For our purposes, it would be foolish to attempt to pinpoint a time when the country changed. Historians might say we lurched from one traumatic event to another.

In television terms, it was the equivalent of a sharp, jolting cut from the Kennedy presidency to the years of civil rights demonstrations – from the murders of Robert Kennedy and Martin Luther King to protests against the Vietnam War.

As these stories of anger and bloodshed were brought into America's living rooms, lives were turned upside down. The civility we once had – however small – was lost as a generation embraced a new culture on the streets and campuses, reflecting the turbulence of the era.

About that same time in broadcasting – the peacefulness of a Sunday morning when television was reserved for religious programs slowly disappeared. There were several programs that viewers followed. Some may still remember on CBS "The Eternal Light" or "Lamp unto My Feet" and other award winning broadcasts.

Now, of course, we have non-stop political shouting programs and other talk shows on the networks and on cable.

The programming has changed.

And – across the years – through tough economic times, wars, national upheavals, and natural disasters, Americans have suffered, but – we've always bounced back.

So, as the pendulum of our lives went from one extreme to another, so did our civility.

It is easy to paint a negative picture of civil life right now – gridlock in Washington, guns on the streets, terrorism, unemployment and foreclosures – just to name a few of our challenges. We have managed to keep a degree of civility, but we can do better.

In order to consider the overall picture of civility, we have to spend a few minutes on reality shows as well as the un-relenting bombardment of information and entertainment from cable channels, the Internet, and bloggers.

Reality shows: your name is Kardashian and your home is on the Jersey Shore.

Turn on the TV and our children are mesmerized by lifestyles that encourage drinking, bad behavior, un-healthy habits and a lack of respect for family values. That's just early in the day.

Evening programming, aimed at a more mature age group, brings us such memorable shows as the real housewives series, mob wives, dance moms, repo men and bridezillas. And there are channels devoted to just about any kind of hobby or strange occupation you want to see.

Of course, there is YouTube – the outlet for video from the sublime to the ridiculous. It's always on and there are people watching all over the world. Unfortunately, I must add – too much of the video on YouTube also finds its way onto news programs just because it is bizarre and usually un-civil. Well, like anything there is good and bad.

Cable and satellite technology does have its positive side. There are many quality channels that are educational and carry programs that are excellent and inspirational. Along with that – we have channels that provide community access and also give us the ability to watch local government in action.

Now, a few words about the Internet, blogosphere and social media.

As someone who has spent his entire life in journalism, I strongly defend freedom of speech. But I believe that civility and truth go hand in hand. So at this point, I want to raise a red flag. When it comes to news – the key question is – what's your source...who told you?

If, as we hear these days, the reply is: I saw it on the Internet – then I add, beware. The Internet is not necessarily the ultimate source for truth. Add the incredible speed of twitter – and news reporters have to be more careful than ever to sort out the truth, to get to the facts.

More often these days, civility disappears on the Internet when it is used as the playground of rumor mongers, and, worst of all, of hateful bloggers and cyber-bullies.

We have all witnessed the dangers attached to social media, mainly the horror of teenagers committing suicide because of cyber-bullying on Facebook. A survey conducted by Consumer Reports last year showed one million children in this country were harassed, threatened or the target of hurtful comments and rumors. Teenage girls were more likely than boys to suffer this unimaginable experience.

Social media is relatively young and has a role to play in society, but it has shown that it must be watched carefully.

At home, we are taught at an early age how to behave in speech and in manners. But media and technology have changed our culture. The violence we see in movies – and "inside" movie theaters – music with demeaning lyrics, tabloid newspapers and television devoting more time to bizarre activities of celebrities – all contribute in some way to a breakdown in society.

Columnist Kathleen Parker, writing in the Washington Post put it this way: "The greatest threat to civility is the pandering to ignorance, the elevation of nonsense and the distribution of false information."

And now, another factor has become part of the equation. A survey of one thousand adults, taken by the public relations firm Weber Shandwick found the level of civility has been made even worse by the on-going financial crisis. Forty-nine per cent of those questioned also consider American CEOs uncivil. Given the Madoff scandal and the low level of trust in Wall Street, they certainly have a point.

At the same time, the survey showed 81 per cent of Americans hold the news media responsible for improving the way we treat each other.

And so, in these early years of the 21st century we are faced with a serious challenge. We must find ways to turn down the volume of our national discourse and stop rewarding bad behavior overall and certainly by celebrities who fail as role models for our children.

Those of us in the media – especially in the news business – have an obligation to society to clear the air.

Adults want that. Even kids look for it.

So in response to hundreds of comments from adults and young people about the shortage of positive news stories, I wrote an upbeat children's book called – *Ernie and the Big Newz, the Adventures of a TV Reporter.* The book is about career choices, believing in yourself – and it is filled with news stories that all have positive endings. Let me explain more about my thinking.

I continually speak at schools throughout our area – and while the feedback and reaction is terrific, it is also eye-opening. Many young children tell me that they feel the only way they can become part of a news broadcast is to do something wrong, do something bad.

It is really no surprise because it is what they see when they watch the news. We mostly reward bad behavior. I believe that kind of thinking has to stop. I am deeply concerned about the unfortunate news events we cannot control that we must report on and its impact on everyone, especially children.

My respected fellow colleagues and I know it's a tough job covering a very fast moving and traumatic world. Today, my message is clear – not all news is negative and living by the golden rule is not old-fashioned.

When it comes to civility in society – and particularly in the media, I am very uneasy about the kind of world we will leave our children.

So, ask me: Are we on the wrong path when it comes to civility in the media?

From what we heard and have seen – the answer is yes.

Well then, can we turn things around and improve the situation? Again, the answer is yes.

So, what do we need to do? Allow me to offer some thoughts:

First, in this media-driven society we have to take the lead by producing more high-quality local programs.

And we have to exercise good editorial judgment when it comes to news stories for our daily broadcasts. How many times do you tune in and a broadcast starts with crime – a child being shot, a teenager with a bright future picked up with drugs, the mugging of an elderly person.

The old tabloid saying goes: "If it bleeds, it leads." in my opinion, that's the wrong approach and it exists only because there's a long-held belief in our industry that it will increase ratings. Many of us believe it doesn't work anymore.

After anchoring close to fifteen thousand newscasts, I've come to the conclusion – people want information that impacts their lives: Is my job in jeopardy? Are food prices going up? Are my children healthy? Are the schools safe? The audience is changing and we must change with it. There is something we can do.

In my career, I've also been in a few Hollywood movies playing the role of a TV news anchor. So a few words about the big studios and production companies are in order.

With all the glitz and glamour, we are still getting more than our share of films that can leave moviegoers with the wrong ideas.

After that horrible shooting in Aurora, Colorado, studio giant Harvey Weinstein of Miramax called for a summit meeting of producers to talk about movie content. We thank him for that and, I fully support this kind of discussion – and hopefully, action.

On a grass roots level, I am urging educators throughout the country to recognize the importance of this issue. For example, they could require students to take a course in media studies to better understand our culture and choose wisely.

I do not want this to become a one-person crusade. So, I am respectfully asking my colleagues in television news, at local stations everywhere to join me. Together we can make this a national effort to improve the balance in the choice of more positive stories on television.

My personal efforts go one step further.

I have recently created a new series of television specials called, "Positively Ernie." We feature refreshing segments on health, education, philanthropy, technology, media – and a wide range of subjects on what's making our community, our country – and even the world – a better place. The feedback has been great.

Finally, we must focus on home family life. Communications is at the center and we need to talk with our children – and really listen.

We also have to connect and strengthen ties with many reputable organizations to do whatever we can to help parents guide children in their use of the internet, social media and TV viewing.

These are a few steps we can all take that can make a difference.

Make no mistake. We have a long way to go. It will not be easy. And it won't happen overnight. But, I am confident that by working together, we can successfully spread the message that civility is the foundation of our lives – and in the media as well.

Stay positive.

ABOUT THE AUTHORS

Francis Thomas "Fay" Vincent, Jr. (born May 29, 1938) is a former corporate lawyer and sports executive who served as the eighth Commissioner of Major League Baseball from September 13, 1989 to September 7, 1992. Vincent played football and baseball as a young man, and was a promising college football player when a near fatal accident in college resulted in a broken back and paralysis.

His roommate in a prank locked him inside his Williams College dorm room. He climbed out to the roof to escape, but slipped off a fourth floor ledge.

Vincent spent many months in the hospital and with physical therapy was eventually able to walk again. But Vincent's mobility has never been fully regained and he uses walking supports.

Vincent is a graduate of The Hotchkiss School, Williams College, (class of 1960), from which he graduated with honors, and Yale Law School (class of 1963). Vincent was a partner in the Washington, D.C. law firm of Caplin & Drysdale for 10 years before becoming president and CEO of Columbia Pictures Industries.

In 1988 he joined his good friend Bart Giamatti in Major League Baseball and became the Commissioner when Giamatti suddenly passed away in 1989.

Dr. Allan E. Goodman is the sixth President of the Institute of International Education, the leading not-for-profit organization in the field of international educational exchange and development training. IIE conducts research on international academic mobility and administers the Fulbright program sponsored by the United States Department of State, as well as over 250 other corporate, government and privately-sponsored programs. Since its founding in 1919, the Institute has also rescued scholars threatened by war, terrorism, and repression. Rescued scholars and other alumni of Institute-administered programs have won 68 Nobel Prizes.

Edward T. Reilly has been the 17th President and Chief Executive Officer of the American Management Association International since June 2001. He is also the Editor of the successful book, "AMA Business Boot Camp," which has been translated and published around the world. AMA (amanet.org) is the world's leading not-for-profit membership-based management development, research and publishing organization. AMA directly interacts each year with over 100,000 executives and managers in the U.S. and around the world through its renowned management education seminar programs. It publishes many newsletters, research papers and a quarterly management journal. AMA produces hundreds of webcasts and podcasts that reach over a quarter million managers around the world. Through its publishing arm, AMACOM, it publishes over 50 books per year and is allied with publishers in over 25 countries.

Ed previously served as President and Chief Executive Officer of Big Flower Holdings, Inc., a leading provider of integrated marketing and advertising services. Prior to joining Big Flower Holdings, he spent more than 25 years with the book publishing and broadcast groups of The McGraw-Hill Companies.

Currently, Ed serves on the following Boards: Member and immediate past Chairman of the USO World Headquarters Board of Governors; Fellow of the International Academy of Management; Member of the U.S. Advisory Board of IESE Business School –

University of Navarra, Barcelona, Spain; Fellow and past Chairman of the Royal Society of Arts in the U.S..

Ed Hold a Bachelor's Degree in Business Administration from St. Francis College, New York and attended the Stanford Executive Program.

Georgia Nugent, a Classics scholar, was the President of Kenyon College from 2003 to 2013 and later a Senior Fellow at the Council of Independent Colleges. Ms. Nugent has held administrative positions at Princeton University and been a professor of Classics at Swarthmore College, Princeton University and Brown University. A member of the first class of women to graduate from Princeton, she later became the first alumna appointed to Princeton's faculty. She took her Ph.D. in Classics at Cornell University. Ms. Nugent, who has received numerous teaching awards, speaks frequently on issues of higher education leadership, as well as the relevance of the Greek and Roman Classics to contemporary society.

James Cuno has been the Chief Executive Officer and President at The J. Paul Getty Trust Inc. since August 2011. A national and international museum leader and scholar, Mr. Cuno was president and Eloise W. Martin Director of the Art Institute of Chicago before joining the Getty. Prior to directing the Art Institute of Chicago, he was the director and professor of the Courtauld Institute of Art, University of London, from 2003 to 2004; the Elizabeth and John Moors Cabot Director of the Harvard University Art Museums and professor of the history of art and architecture at Harvard from 1991 to 2003; director of the Hood Museum of Art, Dartmouth College, from 1989 to 1991; director of the Grunwald Center for the Graphic Arts, UCLA, from 1986 to 1989; and assistant professor of art, Vassar College, from 1983 to 1986. Mr. Cuno serves as a Director of After School Matters, Inc. Mr. Cuno received his A.M. and Ph.D. in the History of Art from Harvard in 1980 and 1985, respectively; an M.A. in the History of Art from the University of Oregon in 1978; and a B.A. in History from Willamette University in 1973.

William J. Bratton was appointed the 42nd police commissioner of the City of New York by Mayor Bill de Blasio, the second time he has held the post.

Commissioner Bratton established an international reputation for re-engineering police departments and fighting crime in the 1990s. As Chief of the NYC Transit Police, Boston Police Commissioner, and in his first term as NYC Police Commissioner, he revitalized morale and achieved the largest crime declines in the city's history. At the NYPD in 1994 and 1995, he led the development of Compstat, the command accountability system now used by police departments nationwide. As Los Angeles Police Chief from 2002 to 2009, in a city known for gang culture and youth violence, he brought crime to historically low levels, greatly improved race relations, and reached out to young people with innovative police programs. He is the only person ever to lead the police agencies of the nation's two largest cities.

A Vietnam veteran, Bratton began his career in 1970 as a beat cop in the Boston Police Department, receiving its top award for valor in 1976 for facing down a bank robber and rescuing a hostage. By 1980 became Superintendent of Police, the BPD's highest sworn position.

A noted author, commentator, and consultant, Bratton holds a bachelor's degree from Boston State College and is a graduate of

the FBI National Executive Institute. He was a Senior Executive
Fellow in Criminal Justice and a member of Harvard University's
Kennedy School of Government's National Executive Session on
Policing. For his collaborative efforts U.S. and British police forces,
he was recognized by Queen Elizabeth II with the honorary title
Commander of the Most Excellent Order of the British Empire
(CBE).

Thomas J. Donohue is president and CEO of the U.S.
Chamber of Commerce. Since assuming his position in 1997,
Donohue has built the Chamber into a lobbying and political
powerhouse with expanded influence across the globe.

During Donohue's tenure, the Chamber's lobbyists, policy
experts, legal advocates, and communicators have helped secure
business victories on Capitol Hill, in the regulatory agencies, in
politics, in courts of law and in the court of public opinion, and
before governments around the world.

In an era of economic and fiscal challenges, Donohue has
aggressively advanced the American Jobs, Growth, and Opportunity
Agenda, a plan that includes expanding trade and domestic energy
production, rebuilding America's infrastructure, combating an
avalanche of new regulations, protecting intellectual property,
revitalizing capital markets, and reforming entitlements and the tax
system.

Donohue has also spearheaded the creation of the Campaign
for Free Enterprise, a positive, long-term program to defend, protect,
and advance the free enterprise system. A signature project of the
campaign is Hiring Our Heroes, which identifies job opportunities
for tens of thousands of returning military veterans and spouses.

Under Donohue's leadership, the Chamber has emerged as a major political force in races for the Senate and the House of Representatives. As part of this bipartisan effort, millions of grassroots business advocates, as well as the Chamber's federation of state and local chambers and industry associations, mobilize in support of pro-business candidates.

Donohue established the U.S. Chamber Institute for Legal Reform, which advances significant legal reforms in the courts, at the state and federal levels, and in elections for state attorneys general and Supreme Court judges. In addition, he has dramatically expanded the activities of the National Chamber Litigation Center, the Chamber's law firm, and the U.S. Chamber of Commerce Foundation.

Previously, Donohue served for 13 years as president and CEO of the American Trucking Associations, the national organization of the trucking industry. Earlier in his career, Donohue was deputy assistant postmaster general of the United States and vice president of development at Fairfield University in Connecticut.

Born in New York City, Donohue earned a bachelor's degree from St. John's University and a master's degree in business administration from Adelphi University. He holds honorary degrees from Adelphi, St. John's, Marymount, and Bradley universities, as well as the National University of Ireland at Maynooth. He is a 2013 recipient of the Horatio Alger Award. Donohue and his wife, Liz, have three sons and five grandchildren.

Georgette Mosbacher, born in Hammond, Indiana, has a BS Degree from Indiana University, and honorary doctorate degrees from Bryant College and the International Fine Arts College. She is the Chairman and CEO of Borghese, Inc., and former owner & CEO of La Prairie, both global personal care companies, the latter she sold to Beiersdorf, Inc.

She is on the Boards of the Atlantic Council, The Intrepid Air Sea and Space Museum, and The Fallen Heroes Fund, and the advisory boards of Brasilinvest, RUSI International, and The Dilenschneider Group. She is founder of the New York Center for Children, and served for a decade as New York State's Republican National Committeewomen. She has served as member of the US Advisory Board for Trade Policy and Negotiations (Presidential appointment) and as a New York Commissioner of Racing (Gubernatorial Appointment) and Trustee of the New York Hudson River Park Trust (Mayoral Appointee). She has authored two best-selling books: *Feminine Force* and *It Takes Money Honey: A Get Smart Guide to Total Financial Freedom*. She is dedicated to our military veterans and their families, to women and children issues, and the furtherance of public private partnerships to solve societal problems.

Joel Irwin Klein is an American lawyer and school superintendent, and was Chancellor of the New York City Department of Education, where he oversaw a system of 1.1 million students and 136,000 employees. While there he led system-wide transformations that resulted in significant increases in student performance. Under Joel's leadership, high-school graduation rates in the City rose 20 points—an increase of more than 40 percent.

A fifth generation Texan, **Governor Rick Perry** has taken an extraordinary Texas journey, from a tenant farm in the rolling West Texas plains to the governor's office of the Lone Star State.

Texas' 47th governor, and the first Texas A&M graduate to occupy the Governor's Mansion, Rick Perry has led a life of public service, starting in the United States Air Force and continuing over two decades in elected office.

Governor Perry's administration has focused on creating a Texas of unlimited opportunity and prosperity by improving education, securing the border and increasing economic development through classic conservative values.

During his tenure, Governor Perry has maintained a strong focus on fiscal discipline, becoming the only Texas governor since World War II to sign budgets that reduced general revenue spending. He has used his line item veto to scrub more than $3 billion in budgeted spending, while encouraging investments in the building blocks of a prosperous state: the economy, education and security.

Former U.S. Sen. Olympia J. Snowe graduated from Edward Little High School in Auburn, Maine. She earned a degree in political science from the University of Maine in 1969. With her election in 1994, Olympia became only the second woman Senator in history to represent Maine, following the late Sen. Margaret Chase Smith, who served from 1949 – 1973. In November 2006, she was re-elected to a third six-year term in the United States Senate with 74 percent of the vote, and served until her retirement in 2013.

Before her election to the Senate, Olympia represented Maine's Second Congressional District in the U.S. House of Representatives for sixteen years. Former Senator Snowe is only the fourth woman in history to be elected to both houses of Congress and the first woman in American history to serve in both houses of a state legislature and both houses of Congress. When first elected to Congress in 1978, at the age of 31, Olympia was the youngest

Republican woman, and the first Greek-American woman, ever elected to Congress. She has won more federal elections in Maine than any other person since World War II.

Ernie Anastos is a distinguished author and Emmy-award winning news anchor for New York City's popular FOX 5 News at 6 pm. He is a champion of promoting more positive news in all aspects of broadcast journalism.

He is a dynamic Hall of Fame Broadcaster with a remarkable record of achievement. Ernie has won more than 30 Emmy awards and nominations, including the prestigious Lifetime Emmy Award and the Edward R. Murrow award for broadcast excellence. The New York Times has described him as "the ubiquitous anchorman" who has captured the love and respect of all New Yorkers.

As a seasoned anchor and reporter, Mr. Anastos has covered major stories throughout his career. On September 11th, he anchored award winning news coverage of the World Trade Center attacks. He has traveled to Cuba, meeting with Fidel Castro and produced a series of special reports on the anniversary of the Cuban revolution. Ernie has also reported on an official pastoral trip traveling to the war-torn countries of El Salvador and Nicaragua.

Made in the USA
Lexington, KY
23 November 2018